Joseph W. Dorr

Babylon

Joseph W. Dorr

Babylon

ISBN/EAN: 9783337243371

Printed in Europe, USA, Canada, Australia, Japan

Cover: Foto ©ninafisch / pixelio.de

More available books at **www.hansebooks.com**

Yours truly,
Joseph W. Dorr.

BABYLON

A HISTORICAL ROMANCE IN RHYME

OF THE TIME OF NIMROD, THE MIGHTY HUNTER-KING; THE TOWER OF BABEL AND THE CONFUSION OF TONGUES.

"THE EVERGREEN SHORE"
"THE HOMESICK PROSPECTOR"
"THE RIDE OF '42"
AND OTHER POEMS.

By JOSEPH W. DORR.

ILLUSTRATED.

TACOMA:
COMMERCIAL PRINTING Co., Publishers,
1897.

PREFACE.

There may be other men in the world who, on the particular subjects touched upon in the story Babylon, have theories as original as those of the writer. There may be men, and women too, who while they have read the old, old story of Adam, of the deluge and of Babel and the King of Salem have been stirred by inspirations as unique and fancies as entertaining as those of sweet Wilda and Gether and their Aryan home. However that may be, the writer has not met with them or heard of them, so his conceptions only owe their existence to the Spirit who gave them paternity. In short Babylon is an inspiration.

This book has not been written for the critics, but for the common people, who are not so cold as they, and more susceptible of sympathy and true affection. Still among the thousands whom I hope will read the story I should be sorry if there should not be some who would apply their minds closely enough to the fabric of the work to discover its fractures of preconceived ideas and legendary notions. It will not require a very close observer to discover the presence of some modern words and terms. The author has a right to enter the plea of ignorance to some extent, if he so desired, of the appellations of archeologists, for he is only a member of the ranks of the common people, but he cares not to take advantage of such a plea and maintains his right to use modern descriptions as he desires. In short, he believes that at the time of the confounding of tongues and building of the tower of Babel that many of the inventions of peace had reached as high a state of perfection as at the present day, which beliefs must explain away any apparent inconsistency in description of implements and other things.

The author is aware also that from a historic standpoint the name Babylon, applied to the city of the tower, can not be as correct as the shorter one, Babel, but when the reader comes to test the two appellations by sound I am sure he will be willing to allow the latitude, and I believe will also permit in the body of the work the technical application of the name Nimrod to the city which the hunter doubtless founded on the ground where afterward stood the more modern city, Babylon.

As to social conditions, there is no doubt in the author's mind that those which led up to the deluge were repeated just prior to the confounding of tongues. Self-seeking—manifested in the accumulation of power and wealth in the hands of the few, and Self-Sufficiency—made manifest by a forsaking of God as an individual personal creator of power and force, and a seeking to investigate by human learning the forces or integral parts of the source of all power. These elements I say, I believe, united to destroy in the first case, and to disrupt, in the second, the worldly social fabric.

As to the characters and plot of the story, as he must in all other points, the author leaves them to the kind mercies of the reader.

There is no necessity, reader, for me to say much in this introduction of the character or inspiration of the other individual parts of this company. You have them; examine them with love, indifference or dislike, as you feel prompted. If you find anything good ascribe it to the Giver above, who giveth every good gift. If these are not lovely in your sight ascribe the

PREFACE.

unloveliness to the failings of human flesh, of which the author admits his share, and try and remember only the comely parts which he only hopes may leave some good impression somewhere.

JOSEPH W. DORR.

Ex. xxxv. 30-35.

DEDICATION.

A tree once grew up by the side of a tall, slender, monument-like rock. It was not so strong as the rock, but it grew and grew until its trunk pressed into the crevasses and its top covered and hid the object which was to be its adamantine supporter. The tree would not have been called beautiful by the thoughtless passer-by, though its fluffy top looked soft and its branches warm and clinging, more like a vine than a tree; and a sweet scented breath blew from it all the while. But one day I planted at its feet the vine of my ideality long-lifed and verdant. Soon the rock and tree were hid in the vernal and clinging folds of this new drapery. Upward it grew until it mingled in the dark tresses of the love which it embraced. If there had been anything unlovely before it was hidden now among the green and rustling leaves and clinging tendrils of my ideality, and I thought as I gazed upon the beautiful fabric of this combination: "If the tree should decay to but a single duct to carry up the stream to support the beauty of its head, by clinging to it and the rock the vine of my ideality would bear it up against the strongest blasts; and if it died would hold its lifeless form in its loving embrace so long as its memory could survive." To the wife of my youth I dedicate this little book.

JOSEPH W. DORR.

CARTE DE GRATITUDE.

When the pencil which wrote most of this little book was worn down until it had to be discarded for a longer one, and the work was about to be submitted to the hands of the printer, a feeling of thankfulness came into the author's heart for the many kindnesses shown him both in spirit and deed, since he commenced the work, and he was prompted to express his gratitude to each individually in this little page, but when he came to recruit their names, he found there were so many kind hearts which had throbbed responsively to his wants that he could not do them each justice, so he will let these poor words express his gratefulness to you all. He knows what you have said and done, for God has blessed him with a good memory, and he remembers his friends and knows no enemies. You know what kindness you have shown him. Please remember it, and appropriate these words of gratitude to yourself just in proportion to the kindness you have felt and shown. He cannot thank you each individually on this page, but he does thank the good Lord for you all, and prays that you may each have the same feeling of kindness toward him and all your neighbors as he has toward you. Believe that the heart impels the inscription of these words by the hand of THE AUTHOR.

BABYLON.

(Reader: Please read the Preface before you begin the story).

PART I.

ARYANA.

Sweet Wilda waded in the brook
Down in a green and sheltered nook.
With sunbeams catching at her hair,
She chased the darting minnows there,
And thus she stirred the limpid stream
This day, a lovely summer dream.
Thus she beguiled these hours of May
Wilda, as fair as any day.
Just budding in her early teens,
Over the pool she deftly leans,
And sees in nature's looking glass
This picture of an Aryan lass;
Eyes of mellow hazel brown,
Looking mid raven ringlets down,
Dimples nestling in each
Velvet cheek of blushing peach.
Form, than supple birch more grace,
Wilda saw below her face.
Pink toes stirred up the yellow sand.
The fish escaped a dimpled hand.
So Wilda waded in the brook,
Nor noticed where the bushes shook,
Nor noticed she the soft footfall,
Or heard the wood bird's gentle call,
But answering to a changing mood,

The grassy bank beneath the wood
Unto her whispering seemed to say:
"Come, maiden, come, oh, come away;"
And then she heard the sparrow's cry,
Within a shady copse hard by,
An answering twitter from her throat,
Seemed on the summer air to float.
And seating her within the shade,
She scanned the road along the glade.
Scarce had the maiden seated her;
Again the bushes gently stir.
A youth bounds out into the space,
And blushes paint fair Wilda's face:
A boy as graceful as the pine,
Replete with beauty masculine;
With bounding life in every move,
A form and face which nourish love.
Bold Gether, none more quick than he
To swim the stream or climb the tree.
In Wilda's girlish eyes a man,
The finest in the caravan,
Or better still, a fresh, free boy,
A sister's pride, a mother's joy.
As hastening to his sweetheart there,
Surely he was to view most fair.
He threw himself upon the sward,
Face all aglow, breath coming hard.
"We missed you, while we wandered down,
"From out our sight and out our sound."
"The water's clearer up the brook,"
The maiden said, with arching look.
He did not deign to note her vein,
But softly spoke to her again:
"I did not care with them to play,
"My Wilda, when you were away."
"Oh, girls are girls and boys are boys."

She said. "and all are full of noise.
"I think that I can hear them now,
"Though they are far away I trow:
"With squeals and shouts they fill the air,
"As though they found some terror there."
 Said he, "I think there's nothing more
"Than some poor crawfish frightened sore,
"To find himself beset about
"By such a din of squeal and shout."
 The maid, as though to tantalize,
 Averting then her dancing eyes,
 Said roguishly: "Kezia fair
"Would safer feel if you were there."
 Then Gether bold, with flushing brow
 And youthful eagerness bent low,
 And whispering to the teasing maid
 As though of other ears afraid:
"Oh, Wilda, why needs mention her,
"You know to me you are most dear.
"No other can your place usurp,
"Where you my idol are set up.
"As this stream runs to the *Green Sea,
"So, Wilda, my love runs to thee,
"And to the spot where flows my love,
"There, too, does then my body move.
"I know Kezia's fair to see
"As any Aryan maid can be,
"But she is not my quiet love,
"My Wilda, forest flower and dove."
 Relenting then the maiden smiled,
 And answered him with accents mild;
"I know it, but how knowest thee
"That this stream runs to the Green Sea?"
"To yonder hill I clambered high,

---

*Ancient name for the Persian Gulf.

"Saw waters stretching to the sky,
"And father says the road we take
"Will lead us by the Aturian lake."
 The maid into a thoughtful mood
 Then glided while her Gether stood
 Waiting to hear her speak again
 When she should gather up her train.
 At last a question on her face,
 As though some mystery to trace,
 With earnestness depicted there:
"Why do we journey thus so far
"From Aryana's dales and hills,
"Her pastures kissed by rippling rills?
"Were we not happy there," she asked
"That now with such a journey tasked?"
 With thoughtful mein he heard her quest.
 With hands beneath his head at rest.
 Then speaking slow and pondering well:
"My Wilda, dear, I cannot tell;
"The journey I so much enjoy
"That I, like any other boy,
"Have never asked the reason why,
"While changing scenes were passing by.
"The traveling days and camping nights
"They are unto my liking quite.
"I think when each bright day is o'er,
"Still golden days stretch out before.
"I know we go to Shinar land,
"But why, I have not tried to find.
"Come when the sun goes down to-night,
"While gathering round the flickering light,
"And ask my father why we go,
"And he will tell us then I know,
"For at the close of every day,
"When evening meal is cleared away,
"We children gather listening round

Wilda, grown to womanhood, as fair as she was sweet and good.

"Our Father, seated on the ground,
"While he some thrilling story tells,
"Which binds us with enchanting spells.
"His stories are the best e'er heard;
"We youngsters never lose a word,
"And I am sure if you were by
"He'd tell us all the reason why
"The Aryian hills we leave behind
"To journey to the western land.
"But listen! here the others come;
"We must prepare for teazing, some,
"For fair Kezia could not live
"If she her pleasantry must hive,
"And Mash, that younger brother mine,
"Could never miss his chances fine
"To plague, if blushes he can raise,
"Or frowns upon his brother's face."
 Wilda, springing to her feet,
 Bounded where the branches meet,
 And as she glided out of sight
 Waved him adieu with motion light.
 Then Gether sauntered to the road,
 Across whose path the brooklet flowed,
 And met the noisy children there,
 Who came, both boys and maidens fair,
 With flowers and shells and pebbles rare;
 Each laden with a generous share,
 Kezia leads the laughing troop,
 Her brow a wreath of flowers held up.
"Oh, Gether, truant, where away
"Have you been hiding all the day?
"One less brave than stout than you
"Would sure have scared us through and through,
"Gliding thus away so still
"While we paddled in the rill.
"In this country strange and new

"Something might have injured you.
"What were you seeking for so long?
"Some bird with strange, bewildering song?"
"Two-footed bird," said little Mash,
"Here I've found her pretty sash."
 Picking up a ribbon bright
 Dropped by Wilda in her flight.
 Then the laughter rang again,
 Giving Gether inward pain,
 But he joined in hearty zest
 In the laughter with the rest,
 Saying (not with angry word)
"Who e'er saw four-footed bird?"
 Fearing search would find her out,
 Gladly he heard a calling shout,
 And it pleased him very well
 Then as rang the dinner bell,
 Driving from all minds away
 Thoughts of truants for the day.
 Then away the children ran,
 Hastening to the caravan,
 Leaving Gether by himself,
 But for Kezia, pretty elf,
 Who more slowly walking here,
 As they to the tents drew near.
 Wilda met them as they went,
 On the ground her glances bent,
 Searching for her truant sash
 Now possessed by little Mash.
"Come," Kezia said, "and dine,
"We know who has your ribbon fine;
"A bird will sometimes lose a quill
"Flying to the forest still."
 And so the trio joined the feast,
 Laughing and talking with the rest.
 All soon forgot the morning's fun;

The day moved toward the setting sun,
And evening drew along apace,
And found the children in their place,
All seated round old Aram's chair,
Eager to each the story hear.
They listen while their bosoms heave
To hear the story he should weave,
Of how this distant march began,
And what caused men this move to plan.
"I fear I cannot do it well
"But for our Wilda I will tell
"As best I can the story long,
"Which reaches back to ages gone.
"So long a time the tale will take,
"I fear you will not stay awake.

PART II.

ARAM'S STORY.

"In *Audyana, when the world was new,
"When men were mighty and the women true,
"Where everything was rich and fresh and fair,
"And nature all adorned with beauty rare,
"Where nothing was offensive or defiled,
"In purity both man and nature smiled,
"The birds sang sweet, the flowers bloomed bright,
"Nor hurt by heat of day nor cold of night;
"Where fruity odor floated on each breeze,
"And nuts bore down the branches of the trees,
"And melons grew and corn and vine,
"And roots e'er rich and tubers fine,
"And milk and honey in abundance flowed,
"And waving wheat by the Creator sowed,

---

*The garden.

"Men were so close to God that they could talk
"With him when he would take his evening walk.
"They were contented then and all secure,
"Their hearts were happy and their thoughts were pure.
"They had their wisdom in their "fear" of God,
"Their knowledge was by keeping in the road,
"Until a day when on their gaze appeared
"One with a story they had never heard,
"Of how men's learning would their lives complete,
"Upraise their minds and guide their groping feet,
"Would make them wise as their Creator was;
"Of all creations they should know the cause,
"And not as children follow his commands,
"But everything control by their own minds.
"He said for disobedience they should not die,
"But into gods should be exalted up on high.
"The woman listened, this was something new,
"So fair the story seemed she thought it true;
"And thus it was that on an awful day
"The mother of our race was led away;
"The fairest queen of all humanity,
"Forgot her God and list'd to sophistry.
"The king, her husband, did with her partake
"To his own woe and God's commandment break,
"And so at last the sad day came about,
"They saw their nakedness and God turned them out
"To till the ground in sorrow and in pain,
"To feel the frosts and fight with driving rain;
"To find what man would do without his God.
"While death lurked in the working weary clod.
"They traveled eastward, lone and sad the day,
"With weary feet they trod the tangled way.
"Scratched by the thorns and pierced by thistles keen,
"They sought for peace and rest in lands unseen.
"Three days they hastened from the blessings lost,

"Until their bodies, sore, demanded rest.
"Mid raging animals and hissing snakes
"They builded them a house of boughs and brakes;
"Their meagre food they dug from out the earth,
"With death on every side they ventured forth.
"For weary months they toiled nor smiled,
"Until in pain God sent a little child,
"Who brought to Eve's sad face the light,
"And nerved up Adam's arm to fight
"Against surrounding ills on every side,
"Lest death should enter in and woes betide.
"And thus they multiplied and filled the earth,
"Encountering threatening death at every birth.
"But sorrowing man could never quite forget
"The blessed place they'd lost, and even yet
"The story's sadly told among the race,
"Of Eve and Adam driven from the happy place.

"As man thus started wrong, he grew
"More wicked as the cumbering ages flew,
"Until at last, God's mighty patience tired,
"Repented him, and sore his anger fired.
"In all the world, though searching sadly through,
"He could not find a human being true,
"Save one, who with his family he'd save,
"Who had a spirit true and honor brave.
"To him he told his awful, fell designs
"To purge the earth of all the wicked of mankind,
"So Noah built an ark against the awful day
"When water should submerge and wash away
"The wicked, selfish, boasting human race,
"Who blasphemed righteousness before his face.
"The ark was finished mid the sneers of men,
"Who said the earth should be as it had been—
"That Noah was demented and befooled,
"And that halucination all his actions ruled.

"The flood came down and drowned the very earth,
"But now in safety Noah floated forth,
"Above the hills, the rocks, the highest trees,
"Above the mountains, wafted by the breeze.
"The ark, with all its load of men and beast,
"Moved slowly off toward the glowing east.
"Seven weary months it floated back and forth,
"Until a wind came blowing from the north
"And dried the cumbering waters off the earth;
"Until the highest mountain tops came forth.
"Then stopped the ark, and quiet sat
"Among the towering peaks of eastern Ararat,
"Just westward from the ancient land of Nod,
"Where Cain went from the presence of his God.
"An altar and burned sacrifice were made.
"And Noah unto God his homage paid.
"With bending knee, and gazing up on high,
"He saw the painted bow across the sky,
"And heard, delighted, (that which gave Hope birth)
"God's promise, never more to drown the earth.

" 'Twas springtime, and the birds and flowers
"Soon decked the valleys down below in bowers,
"But snows were falling on the mountain peak,
"So man commenced the lower plains to seek.
"The ark remained, and there remains to-day,
"Safely preserved and buried in the snow away,
"Till age on age have gone into the past,
"And God reveals its hiding place at last.
"Our people used to climb, a hundred years ago,
"Up to the ark's drear tomb amid eternal snow,
"And walk above its roof, so many cubits down,
"While snowy mountains stood with icy frown,
"Threatening with death the curious climber bold,
"Who dared to face their howling blasts of cold,

"To propagate rem'niscent feeling there,
"Among the frosty drifts and glacier glare.

"As time passed on the memory grew dark,
"With nothing to be seen but outline of the ark,
"With snowy blankets clinging close about
"Its massive form from gopher fashioned out,
"And that was all; its chambers ever hid
"By drifts which bravest burrower defied,
"But still the shrouded shape is ever there.
"Protected from the inroads of decay and wear.

"Well, time wore on, and Jafeth traveled east,
"While Ham, his brother sought the garden west.
"My father stayed and reared his simple home,
"And tilled his fields anear the snowy dome
"Where rested, when the mighty flood was past,
"The ark which bore them safely to its rest.
"And Noah stayed and made his home close by;
"He loved the green hillsides and glowing sky.
"As year by year went by and generations came
"Grandfather thought it meet to give the land a name.
"The valley, rich among the hills so grand,
"With air ethereal was a pleasant land.
"He thought upon the scenes and beauties there,
"The echoing hills and crystal streams so fair;
"Upon the towering snow-clad sentinel,
"And then upon the air ethereal,
"Breathing which thrilled the dancing blood
"And filled the throbbing valves with fluid good,
"Then looking up toward heaven far above,
"And thinking reverently of God's wondrous love,
"He named the new land 'Aryana,' home of pure air;
"And built among the hills a city fair:
" 'Bactriana,' which the world knew well
"As Noah's home and Aryana's capital.

"The people grew and overspread the earth,
"And never had of fruits and grain a derth.
"Their cattle covered over all the hills,
"The valleys echoed with their rumbling mills,
"And all were happy and serene content,
"When on a day not to be soon forgot,
"From Bactriana wondrous news was brought:
"They'd found the place where beauteous Eden was,
"In Shinar, west of Audyana, near to Uz,
"My brother, who was now a father of a land,
"Named for him, a country fair and grand.
"Noah had gone; my brother Asshur, too,
"And so we thought no doubt the story true.
"A king was there most wondrous in the chase
"Bold Nimrod, who before God's face
"A mighty hunter was, and king of power,
"Ruler of the land and hero of the hour.
"Then all the people talked the matter o'er,
"And as time passed the interest grew more.
"On every hand the people talked of naught at all
"But Eden's beauties and of man's sad fall,
"Of this rich land of Shinar in the west,
"Where grains and fruits all grew the very best;
"And as the elders talked, the youngsters, too,
"Grew warm in wonder at the story new,
"And so at last a company was formed
"Of those whose hearts with rapture warmed
"At memory of the old, old story grand,
"Of Eden fair, and of the birth of man.
"The new land, so the pretty story told,
"Was rich as Eden was in days of old,
"With forests sprinkled o'er the verdant hills,
"With rivers grand and many twittering rills.
"And so you all remember how the start began,
"This journey to the western wonder land.
"That we shall strangers be we need not fear

Gether.

"For good old Noah lives, with brother Asshur there
"And Ham, my dark skinned uncle, who so long ago
"Moved toward the setting sun, as you all know,
"Dwells by the river there, and his brave son
"Upon the river banks a city has begun.
"We've traveled twenty days from our old home,
"And there are fifteen days of journey yet to come
"Before we reach the sweet, enchanted place
"Which saw the birthday of the human race.
"We rest a day by this clear crystal brook
"To oil our wagons and revive our stock,
"Then on our journey we again will be
"Along the roadway by the green Green Sea.
"You children shall enjoy the passing hours
"With changing scenes and with birds and flowers.
"But while we have thus at our story been
"The clock in yonder van is striking ten;
"And now I've all the simple story told
"Of why we journey to this country old,
"So now to bed to rest you from your play,
"And thus prepare you for another day
"Now, Wilda, Gether, my brave young man,
"Will see you safely to your father's van."
"Oh, thank you, sir," the gentle maid replied,
"I have your story, oh, so much enjoyed."
Good nights were said, and soon the camp grew still
With all asleep except the rippling rill,
Or the Green Sea, which all the passing night
Sang lullabys until the morning light.

PART III.
NIMROD.

He stood upon the river bank,
   A mighty man was he,
With curling locks and flashing eye
   And form e'er grand to see.

Around him stood admiring crowds,
   Eager to do his will
In toil, or chase, or service mean,
   Or gaze and gaze their fill.

His jetty skin flashed in the sun,
   He stood a giant tall,
In meditation by the stream,
   The people silent all.

They listened speechless by his side
   To hear what he should say.
Eager to hear his least request,
   And anxious to obey.

All day the chase had been pursued,
   Through swamp and forest wide,
And now at evening time they rest
   Upon the river side.

The game piled on the grassy bank,
   Showed skill upon the chase,
And satisfaction sharing with
   Fatigue on every face.

And thus they rested while their chief
   Stood there in revery,

Nor moved a form while ears alert
  An anxious every eye.

But lying on the grass hard by
  Some youths with boyish joy,
Looked with delight upon the game,
  Fruits of the busy day.

Their effervescing life o'ercame
  The universal awe.
And thus they freely talked upon
  The things which now they saw.

And on the most exciting scenes
  Beheld upon the chase,
And told of skill and strength and luck,
  Of swiftness and of grace.

And even they, with praises warm
  Their chief's great prowess owned,
In fiery terms they eulogized
  And passed his name around.

Said one, "I never saw a man
  "So wonderfully quick.
"And I, while in a glade to-day,
  "Saw him outrun a buck.

"He seized by one sharp, flying foot,
  "And held it fast and sure,
"Then let it gladly through the woods
  "Go bounding free once more.

"He would not kill a creature thus
  "While helpless in his power;
"He'd rather give it chance for life,
  "If he must run an hour.

"He'd rather show his own great skill
  "With his unerring gun.
"Than honor Nature all alone,
  "Who gave him power to run."

Another said, "I saw him leap
  "Full thirty feet or more
"Across a streamlet in his path,
  "As on his course he bore.

"He never for an instant slacked
  "Upon his wondrous speed,
"As like a bird he clave the air,
  "Nor to the ground gave heed.

"No man in all the company
  "Could keep his form in sight,
"Though urged by every sense of pride
  "To strive with all his might."

And thus the praise was passed around
  By each admiring youth,
And looking at their hero
  One could never doubt their truth.

With form full eight feet tall he stood,
  Like some great ebon tower,
The muscles of his arms and legs
  All showing mighty power.

A face as powerful as his form,
  Marked with an intellect,
Which, as his body grand, could claim
  Unanimous respect.

And thus he stood, while moved the day
  Toward its twilight grave,

Among his willing subjects still,
　　This king of Shinar brave.

Bold Nimrod had upon his mind
　　Some thought of deep import,
While silence brooded o'er him there,
　　To close this day of sport.

His people listened while he leaned
　　Upon his trusty gun,
Which had that day, with bullet true,
　　Stopped many a red deer's run.

Some weighty plan must be in store
　　To such a silence keep;
They wait expectantly to hear
　　While evening shadows creep.

At last he speaks, his voice was like
　　A lion's evening roar,
They listen silently to hear
　　What Nimrod has in store:

"You'll all admit," said he, "my friends,
　　"That I'm a mighty king
"Of me the people proudly speak,
　　"Of me the minstrels sing.

"No man in all the world can stand
　　"In contests of the chase.
"No hand can set my gun for game,
　　"None keep up in the race
"With me, (while quick springs forth the deer
　　"Upon the vernal sward)
"Or leap the streams beside me
　　"Though trying e'er so hard.

"I do not boast of things unknown
  "When talking of my strength,
"For nature does not give with power
  "Of days a greater length.

"But this I know, my skill has won
  "For me a mighty name,
"And I should hope that something may
  "Perpetuate the same.

"These things are well enough indeed
  "For youth's swift passing days,
"But I've a wish some mark to make
  "My name to live always."

The people shouted, then, with pride,
  "Long live our mighty king!
"Down through the ages yet to come
  "Loud may his praises ring."

A smile of pleasure floated o'er
  Bold Nimrod's ebon face
To hear what he had heard before
  The plaudits of his race.

"I thank you well my followers,"
  Said he with look of pride
"I feel that I can move the world
  "When you stand by my side.

"Now let the camp be set upon
  "The bank hard by us here,
"Where tumbles down from yonder hill
  "The streamlet cold and clear.

"And when the evening's meal is done
  "You'll gather at my tent,

"And listen while I tell to you
  "Indeed my heart's intent."

The funeral of the day came on,
  Dressed in its roseate train,
Which 'flected in the river's face
  And over wood and plain.

And soon 'twas buried dark away
  Within the fields of night.
With naught to cheer the hunter's camp
  But flickering gleams of light,
Or some sweet note from Jubal's flute,
  Which looed from singer's tent,
While those who cooked the evening's meal
  Were at their employ bent.

Soon sounds the call from Nimrod's door,
  His followers gather there.
That they may listen at his feet,
  His great designs to hear.

"My purpose," said the mighty one,
  "In choosing here my camp,
"Was not to 'scape the drouth of plain,
  "Or marsh or river damp,
"But here, beside this river grand,
  "Upon this grassy knoll.
"I hope with brick and stone to build
  "A mighty capital.

"Erich and Accad, places fair,
  "Adorn the Shinar plains,
"And Calneh, by the river brink,
  "A queen of cities reigns,
"But I would here a city build

" Of wide and worthy fame,
"Which should, a monument for aye,
　"Perpetuate my name."

" 'Tis well, 'tis well," the people shout,
　"We'll build it wide and high,
"The grandest city in the world,
　"E'er seen by mortal eye,
"And for our king we'll name it, too,
　"And worthy shall it be,
"A monument to stand for aye
　"For such an one as he.

"While other cities may be fair,
　"And great, and good and grand,
"Nimrod shall be the king of all,
　"The greatest in the land.

And the Euphrates glided by
　To meet the green Green Sea,
While Nimrod's camp slept on its banks,
　The moon rose silently.

A dark and towering form stole forth
　To walk upon the sand,
And pacing up and down the shore,
　His works for future planned.

Soliloquizing as he walked,
　The form passed to and fro,
And let us come and walk with him,
　And listen while we go.

"This is the place where Eden was,"
　He muttered on the night,
"This is where once the tree of life
　"Flourished in God's own sight.

" 'Tis fitting that a monument
  "To one so blessed as I,
"In this the birthplace of mankind,
  "Should be raised up on high.

"Here Adam walked, a perfect man,
  "Amid bright nature new,
"Here, in this very spot he slept
  "When God made woman too.

"Here Cush, my father, pitched his tent,
  "And Ham, his father lived,
"When out from Aryana they
  "With all their chattels moved.

"A monument to me would be
  "A monument to them,
"And thus a treble purpose serve,
  "This city to my name.

"This place reserved three hundred years
  "In virgin beauty rare,
"Shall have a name which shall endure
  "Wherever mortals are."

And so bold Nimrod paced the earth
  While sound his followers slept,
And they ne'er dreamed while slumbering
  Their king the night watch kept.

When morn chased back with smiling brow
  The shadows of the night,
The hunters back to Calneh marched
  Filled with their project quite.

And thus it was, while time went by
  That Nimrod's walls were raised,

And on her palaces and streets
   The world with rapture gazed.

And Shem from Ayriana came
   And Noah, too, was there,
To walk the fields of Eden o'er
   And see the city fair.

And Tera, with his handsome son,
   Whose name was Abraham,
When he became the father
   Of the race which bore the Lamb.

The world ne'er heard such mighty names
   As graced bold Nimrod's court,
And waited for his look and call
   To come to his support.

And there was Nimrod city built
   Upon Euphrates' banks,
And people from the Aryan world
   Came there to swell its ranks.

And man grew wise in his own eyes
   And thought to make God's secrets his;
He thought the means he could devise
   And by his wits accomplish this.

PART IV.

THE SPIRITS OF SHINAR.

The spirits of Shinar were mighty and ruled
Mankind with o'erweening presumption and gold,
Those spirits, were, too, both repulsive and tyre,
But conceit, in their own eyes, had made them most
   fair.

Selfishness said, "I will work for my own;
"I'll have gold for my hire, or let work alone,
"No impulse for love or for principle moved
"Shall ever among men stand boldly approved.

"But unless there is gold for each trivial deed
"No ear shall be touched or to pleadings give heed,
"But 'how much is the pay?' shall spring to the lips,
"As the chance for a loving act silently slips."

Then Learning stood up with an arrogant air,
And said, with a smile, "your wealth we will share,
"For myself with your money can anything do,
"In heaven above or in earth down below."

So they wriggled themselves in to each human soul,
Until one or the other all actions control,
Till the people of Shinar no impulses knew,
But were moulded and shaped by one of these two.

And Pity seemed dead in the hearts of all men,
And Love, with her tears, long in silence had been,
For "the fittest," who ruled, only schemed for their own,
And the poor made to suffer in silence alone.

And Nimrod grew grander, the pride of the world,
And the great in her streets in their vanity whirled
One half of the people in luxury rolled,
While the others were grovelling slaves unto gold.

And selfishness ruled, a despot supreme,
In the hearts of the great who had no other dream
Than to make more secure their wealth and their pride,
While the truth from the masses they'd constantly hide.

And this was the state when a meeting was called
By Nimrod, the king, and the city was filled,
With people from every village and plain,
Who came to greet Nimrod through sunshine and rain.

A vast congregation they gathered at last
In the great council hall a company massed,
Awaiting the coming of Nimrod the Great,
Who should royally lead the vast meeting in state.

His notable subjects awaited with awe,
Their monarch's appearing; his wish it was law.
The last had scarce settled himself in his seat,
When up the broad stairway came tramping of feet.

Then Nimrod came in at the head of his train,
A company worthy his wonderful reign.
The men were all giants in stature, and each
Dressed in raiment as soft as the blush on a peach.

But were they all princes, perfect to a man,
Nimrod was well worthy to lead in the van,
For his stature was grander and stronger than theirs,
As proud through the throng his great head he bears.

Clothed in a suit of soft, close-fitting gray,
Each subject instinctively cleared him the way.
As his muscles stretched tightly the folds of the cloth,
Over shoulders and breast and arms and legs both.

Thus, the simplest form in his bright colored train,
Yet all would have chosen his figure to reign.
So up the soft carpets he walked to the boards,
Which raised, a full view of the people affords.

Then the concourse arose as if one mighty form,
And a shout rent the air like a fierce mountain storm.
Hats and scarfs filled the air as from some mighty loom,
Which was raining down fabrics all over the room.

But the tumult was hushed when thrice it had swelled,
Till the walls of the building were scarcely upheld,
Then Nimrod arose from his throne, and again
The throng raised its voice like the wind on the plain.

Then the people grew eager for what he should say,
And silence fell down while the sound floats away.
A mouse running over the carpets of plush
Would have surely disturbed in the terrible hush.

Not one but well knew in that audience vast
That something of import would come at the last.
The king had not lightly assembled his court,
But his word, when he spoke, should some vast plan report.

"I am told," said the king, "that science has made
"Some wondrous disclosures from heaven, 'tis said.
"Our scholars have learned there are secrets above,
"Which humans can grasp if their means they approve.

"They say with a building sufficiently high
"The skill of the scholar can drag from the sky
"The secrets which only Jehovah now knows,
"And plain to the gaze of all humans disclose.

"We hope a great sctructure to rear to the cloud,
"To make us a name on the record e'er proud.
"We'll build it of brick with walls thick and high
"And from it we'll study the face of the sky.

"What say you my friends?" said the great hunter
    king,
"Shall we set now to labor and do this great thing?
" 'Twill be a day's wonder for gods and for men,
"And help us most valuable learning to win."

A man of few words, Nimrod soon took his seat,
When up rose each man in the room to his feet;
The band began playing, "Long, Long, Live the
    King,"
And the music and cheering made the old arches
    ring.
"We'll build it! we'll build it!" they shout with one
    voice,
"And more we will do for the king of our choice:
"We'll make us a name for the world to admire,
"We'll labor for Nimrod, and never shall tire."

And so it transpired that an edict went forth
Over Shinar that month east and west, south and
    north,
That the laboring people from forty years down
To thirty should gather at Nimrod in June,
To toil for the state in building the tower,
Receiving for wages a penny, no more.

The chief ones decided that clothing and food,
For laboring people, was ample and good,
And if they received a few pennies beside,
They certainly then should be quite satisfied.

But one voice in Shinar was raised for the poor,
When Asshur would have of the follies no more,
And marched with his flocks and his people as well
To a place he would seek in the north land to dwell.

Old Noah bewailed the distress of the poor,
And predicted God's curse on the people once more.
Our Gether and Abram, his choice bosom friend,
Oft conversed with the patriarch learned and kind,
Who could tell of the flood and the ruin of man,
By the vain self-assurance to which he had run.

And Wilda, Sweet Wilda, of whom we have heard,
Oft showed her kind heart both by act and by word.
She sorrowful grew, for it troubled her sore
To see the sad lot of the suffering poor.

But the great work went on with these protests so few
That the king in his glory and pride never knew,
And black and white mingled in pride to behold
With great admiration a project so bold.

They builded each balcony higher and higher,
And up to the heavens began to inspire.
Queen Jemima rode gay in her chariot so grand,
All round the great tower, her chargers in hand.
Her face than a lily more beauteously fair,
Her form covered up with her glorious hair,
Which flowed like a torrent of gold to her waist,
A creature exquisite in beauty and grace.

One day as she rode to the top of the pile,
Her face rippling o'er with a proud, selfish smile,
A laborer chanced from the top of the wall,
By a slip of the hand to let a brick fall,
Which struck with a crash in its lightning descent,
And a hole in the top of the chariot rent,
The queen in her anger declared in a rage
The culprit must then be hurled down from the stage.
No matter, though pleading for mercy he'd cry,

The man for example must miserably die.
So selfish had come the great people to be,
That their queen with indifference such misery could
    see.

But the building went forward, and with it the power
Of learning and selfishness grew as the tower,
Until, in their pride, men declared they were gods,
Who would grasp and control both the winds and the
    floods.

PART V.

BABEL.

God saw the tower approach the sky,
    And heard the boasts of men,
And said "these vain imaginings
    "Quite long enough have been."

A frown was clouding o'er his brow,
    His heart with anger wrung;
"I'll touch," he said, "bewilderingly,
    "These people in the tongue.

"Left to themselves they'll never cease
    "From nothing be restrained
"Until the deepest secrets
    "They have for themselves obtained.

"They are mighty here in Shinar,
    "And with e'er increasing power,
"And ambition overweening,
    "They have thought to build this tower.

"My poor are here oppressed amid
  "This splendor and this wealth,
"And selfishness has crept among
  "The people as by stealth.

"Until their each and every aim
  "Is to delight the rich,
"While they oppress my helpless poor
  "Down to the meanest pitch.

"And even they, while grovelling,
  "Are willing if they can,
"To rise above their fellows
  "By the favor of some man;

"And then join in the struggle,
  "While trampling down their race,
"For the honors and indulgings
  "Bought with power and pelf and place.

"Thus the battle rages onward,
  "With no end to greed and guile,
"And their spirits never upward
  "But go downward all the while.

"Though their wealth and learning groweth,
  "And their power extendeth wide,
"Folly does the simplest lessons
  "From their groping senses hide.

"And the spirit of right living,
  "Buried out of sight complete,
"While with ever eager craving
  "Men for place and power compete.

"From the fields of Aryana,
  "Mid the pastures pure and green,
"To the turmoil here in Nimrod,
  "Seeking prestage man has been.

"Till he thinks he now has found it,
  "In the learning and the gold
"Of this city by the river,
  "Ruled by mighty Nimrod bold.

"He forgets how man was lifted
  "From the dust to form and life,
"How when lonely there in Eden,
  "We prepared for him a wife.

"How he fell, and to the eastward
  "Was in sorrow driven forth,
"How he peopled all the country,
  "From the south unto the north.

"How he grew in power and numbers,
  "How he then the earth defiled,
"While we favored him with chances,
  "And both heaven and nature smiled.

"Though old Noah whispers warnings,
  "All among them here to-day,
"They forget how we in anger
  "Washed their wicked works away.

"But they now in vain imaginings
  "Seek to snatch from us our power,
"And about the streets go boasting,
  " While they're raising up this tower.

"So we'll scatter them abroad then,
  "O'er the whole earth far and wide,

"Some shall in the desert wander.
  "Some shall in the forest hide.

"Some shall seek the torrid rivers,
  "Some shall seek the inland sea,
"And the islands others people,
  "Mid the waves their home shall be.

"Some shall cross the rolling ocean;
  "To a new world now unknown,
"Some in companies shall travel,
  "Others wander all alone.

"North and south unrest shall drive them,
  "East and west their paths shall wind,
"Still shall be that awful longing,
  "Something better they may find.

"None shall find the rest they seek for
  "Till they meet the Purchaser,
"And with him have held sweet council,
  "Till their souls with love shall stir."

  It was heaven's own day in Shinar,
    And the sky with deepest blue,
  Hung above sweet eager nature,
    Freshly washed in morning dew.

  Birds songs came from out the woodlands,
    And among the meadows green,
  Bobolinks a swinging, singing,
    On the gum weeds might be seen.

  To the sea the great Euphrates
    Glided over silver sands,

Gave the thirsty meadows waters
   Fresh from God's own kindly hands.

All the world seemed glad and happy,
   As beheld the summer sun,
While fresh nature rose to greet him,
   And the daily tasks begun.

But in man's great mart were weary
   Thousands toiling on the tower
Who ne'er heard the happy bird songs,
   Saw the sweetly blooming flower.

Never listened to the gurgle
   Of the mossy woodland brook,
Or for restful recreation
   Sought the peaceful sylvan nook.

Nimrod's streets grew thronged with busy
   Thousands passing on their way,
While the sun moved up majestic
   Toward the pinnacle of day.

Rang the hammer, klinked the trowel,
   Creaked the whirling lifting wheels,
Rang the shouts of many drivers,
   Pushing hard the straining heels.

Brick by brick the tower is rising
   To the high pavilion top,
High above the clouds, low hanging,
   Where the mighty work shall stop.

Round the balconies ascending,
   Nimrod's chariot appears,

He the mighty work contemplates.
  He the busy turmoil hears.

See the sun approach the zenith,
  Soon from mouth to mouth will go
Loud to all the noonday order,
"To the dining court below."

On the highest peak stands Nimrod,
  Straight toward the earth the sun
Points his gleaming fire-tipped light spears,
  And the half day's work is done.

Silent on the topmost apex
  Of the day the sun stands still,
For one awful thrilling moment,
  Then strange shouts the heavens fill.

Swelling on the winding pathways,
  Mid the courts and from the earth,
To the very peak, and Nimrod,
  One wild yell comes bursting forth.

Forms are swarming from the doorways,
  Strange wild waving arms appear,
Subtle spells have filled the people,
  Wrap their giant king with fear.

Waiting stands the chariot driver,
  For the king to point the way,
By a word, the course to follow,
  Thus to end their lofty stay.

Downward winds the dizzy pathway,
  Clinging to the massive sides,

Like some serpent close enfolding,
  As towards his prey he glides.

From the artificial mountain
  Pour the busy toilers out,
And their mingling cries ascending
  Reach Nimrod, one mighty shout.

Thus they swarm the winding driveway,
  Like a hive of maddened bees
Stirred by some mischievous youngster,
  Thus in wanton vein to tease.

Patiently the driver listens
  For the word to reach his ear,
For the word to turn his chargers,
  For the word he shall not hear.

Watching close his master's visage,
  There he sees an ashen hue
Stealing over cheek and forehead,
  Caused by some sensation new.

Stirs the king some fearful feeling,
  Shakes his mighty towering form,
Filling full the faithful driver
  With a nameless new alarm.

Still in silence Nimrod frowning
  Sits in fearful trembling there,
As though held by some strange magic
  In some unseen mighty snare.

Then at last the king arising,
  Madly waves his hand about,

And some strange articulation
  Do his trembling lips give out.

Turns the driver all uncertain,
  To pursue the downward way,
Slowly step the prancing horses,
  As though longing there to stay.

Then a look of rage and terror
  Stormed across the monarch's face,
Yelling like some strange wild creature,
  Leaped he to the driver's place.

With one mighty sweep then Nimrod
  Dashed the trembling man aside,
Seizing wildly reins and whipstock,
  Thus commenced the downward ride.

Looking upward frightened faces
  Saw the dusky monarch come,
Sweeping down the narrow driveway
  Like some maddened creature dumb.

Round the circling balcony rushing
  Madly lashed the steeds the king,
Fleeing from before his chargers.
  See his subjects hastening.

As he wildly passes by them,
  Hears he no familiar words,
All are jabbering some strange jargon,
  Like a flock of chattering birds.

Each one fleeing from his neighbor,
  Each one of himself afraid,

As he finds his tongue unruly,
   And his thoughts thus not obeyed.

Each one feels himself demented,
   While he knows his neighbor mad,
And each flees from what, he knows not,
   To escape some spirit bad.

All forgot the tower they builded,
   While they hastened wild away,
As the sun commenced descending
   Down the western slope of day.

King and subjects thronged the highways,
   Screaming, babbling the while,
And the air was filled with tumult.
   Every one had ceased from toil.

Each one madly, wildly rushing
   North and south and east and west.
Language by them all forgotten,
   They had learned at mother's breast.

None to converse, none to counsel,
   None to them a word could speak,
Though among the wise and simple
   Throughout Nimrod they should seek.

Thus the sun went down on Nimrod,
   On a scene of terror wild,
Calls and screams and frantic rushing
   Were not by the midnight stilled.

Wild scared faces ever peering,
   Ears that listened for one word,

Sound artic'late in the darkness,
  That familiar might be heard.

At the sunrise weak and weary,
  None had found the golden key,
Which should by some magic turning
  Open wide the mystery.

But, as though by some strange instinct,
  People gathered two by two,
Guided by some gentle spirit,
  Sent from somewhere, no one knew.

Pair by pair the men and women
  Mated, grasped each other's hand,
As they seemed, by some strange instinct,
  To each other understand.

Children, who had wildly crying
  Ran about the roaring town,
Seemed by instinct drawn to people
  They had never even known.

Thus they gathered into families,
  Speaking each in separate tongue,
And in groups commenced to wander
  From the city streets among.

Nimrod's queen a lab'rer 'compnied,
  Who with skin Sematic white,
Seemed her babbling to interpret,
  She his words divining quite.

Nimrod sought a plebian woman,
  With a skin as black as night,

Both seemed happy and contented,
 Fair within each others sight.

To the westward moved the black man,
 Sons of Canaan, to a land
By the great sea there to linger
 Near the unknown world beyond.

But their destiny should lead them
 To the south, where they should be
Planted neath the tropic verdure,
 Peopl'ing Ethiopia.

God looked down from heaven on Nimrod,
 While its people marched away,
Said, we'll call this city 'Babel,'
 "From this strange and awful day."

So it was the people scattered,
 With their flocks and herds apart,
For to build the tower of Babel
 Never more had they the heart.

God had there their tongues confounded,
 And from there would scatter them,
Over all the earth to wander,
 Until peopled it became.

PART VI.

MELCHIZEDEK.

Sweet Wilda, by the cottage door,
Beheld the sun in heaven soar,
Until it stood straight over head,
And all the morning hours had fled.

Her father by her on the stoop,
Toward the glowing sun glanced up,
"Well, half the day is gone," said he,
"A day of import it will be,
"For Noah says that God will come
"At midday down the heavens from,
"And for the selfishness of man
"Will meet out punishment again.
"He sees the folly of the tower,
"The grandeur of King Nimrod's power.
"With language one they scheme and plan
"For deeds that ne'er belong to man,
"Nor heed the suffering of the poor,
"But reach for wealth and power the more.
"To-day at noon they'll finish then
"The course of folly they have run,
"For God will then their tongues confound
"And scatter them the world around.
"The city's name no more will be
"Nimrod, grand and great to see,
"But from the strange confounded speech
"Which God has given unto each,
"It's name from hence will "Babel" be—
"To-day its fall shall surely see."

Wilda, grown to womanhood,
As fair as she was sweet and good,
Looked sadly down the beauteous street
As though some form her gaze should greet.
She gazed awhile, then turned and said,
"Oh, father, such things make me sad,
"How can men be so very bad?
"How can they thus in selfishness
"Forget that only God can bless;
"And tread the rights of others down
"While seeking to extend their own?

"And oh, I fear that Gether, too,
"Has, with the others, tried to do
"Some selfish things to him quite new.
"I should be shocked indeed if he
"Should mutter some strange words to me,
"When next I meet him at the door.
"My heart would be quite sad and sore
"If he, when we this evening meet,
"With unknown tongue my welcome greet.

Thus they conversed as moments flew,
What things were passing neither knew,
Until upon the listening ear
A horrid shrieking sound drew near;
Sounds in their street ne'er heard before,
Which brought them quickly to the door.
Old Nahor on his daughter leaned,
And with his hand his eyes he screened;
Then both beheld a fearful sight,
Which to their minds was awful quiet.
The king's barouche swept down the street
With mighty Nimrod on the seat,
In some strange tongue he cursed his steeds,
And neither man nor creature heeds,
But standing upright in his place,
Yelling he keeps his awful pace.
His steeds soon bore him out of sight,
But Wilda felt an awful fright,
For from the city all about
She heard one frightened, groaning shout,
Which like some cry of agony,
Seemed reaching quite unto the sky.
Then running to and fro began;
There seemed a fear in every man,
And ladies, too, with faces fair,
Ran through the streets with streaming hair,

And searched about with weary feet,
For some one who would kindly greet
With words that they could understand,
Or kindly take them by the hand.
And many youths, and children, too,
Sought wildly for some one they knew,
For those most near by ties of home
Had now to each strangers become.
And homes whose only tie was pride
Flew wildly from each others' side.
'Twas true, and still they knew it not,
The only true tie to be got
Was love, which could interpret thought.
And only mutual love could make
These strange new sounds a meaning take.
And so it was that husbands, wives,
Who pride had made to guide their lives,
Found they were strangers quite to each
In this strange jumbling of speech.
And thus the streets were filled with cries,
With aching limbs and straining eyes,
For all rushed wildly to and fro
To catch a sound that they would know.
The rich, the poor alike were there,
Both men of might and ladies fair.
There was in this no favor shown,
Save unto those who love had known,
And such each other's language knew
And each to each clung fast and true.

At evening Wilda took her seat
Where she could look adown the street,
And watched with longing in her heart
For him who seemed of life a part.
She saw the sun retire to rest,
And saw him kiss the river's breast;

And still no Gether came to greet
His waiting love for converse sweet.
The dusk had hung the curtains round,
And tears came up from out the ground.
But still sweet Wilda waited there
For him her evening watch to share.
The pale moon rose beyond the tower,
Reminding her how late the hour.
Her father had retired to rest,
With spreading hands his daughter blessed.
All round their home was calm and still,
Yet from the streets came callings shrill.
Of some poor soul who sought a mate,
E'en though the hour was growing late;
And Wilda waited, hoping yet
That Gether would not her forget,
But some sweet spirit would him guide
Until he reached her waiting side.
Despite his tongue, entangled now
Till he could not remember how
To speak the name of she who loved,
Although his heart had selfish proved.

At last a step was drawing nigh,
And Wilda breathed an anxious sigh
And wondered if he'd pass her by.
Could it be he who's step she heard—
So strangely slow it scarcely stirred;
Like some aged footman, wearied quite
With toiling from the morn till night?
But while she wondering, hoping sat
A tall form stopped beside the gate,
And though he uttered not a sound,
Sweet Wilda met him with a bound;
For oft' she'd played in field and wood,
With he who silent, waiting stood,

In years gone by when children, they
Claimed for their own each golden day.
In Aryana far away.
In he who sadly waited there
She saw a boy with curling hair,
Who early won her girlish heart;
Whose presence made her pulses start
With keener sympathy to-night,
(As she with sorrow saw his plight)
Than even when, as girl and boy,
They spoke their vows between their play.

"Oh, Gether," sadly murmured she;
Some unknown jargon muttered he.
His tongue refused to shape her name,
Could not a word familiar frame.
She knew the hand of God had hung
An instant over Gether's tongue,
And changed his understanding so,
That what she said he could not know.
A flood of thought came to her then,
Of what their youthful lives had been.
She could not lose her Gether now,
She must devise some method how
She might her lover teach to speak,
And thus this awful thraldom break.
She would be patient, kind and mild
And teach him like a little child.
Though years of struggle should be passed,
She'd surely free his tongue at last;
And speak such words his ears to woo,
That he should all her meaning know.
They sat there till the hour had quite
Sank downward to the pit of night.
Down where the willows dipped their hands,
Above Euphrates' yellow sands,

The nightingale in plaintive note
Expressed her sorrows from her throat.
But Wilda's heart was sadder still,
Than any night bird's lonely trill.

The cricket creeked beneath the step,
With sound above the river's sweep,
And every whispering, dancing sprite
Was hastening to the lunch of night.
The owl called down the accents low,
And Gether slowly rose to go.
He moved in a bewildered way,
As though he would not go or stay,
But Wilda softly took his hand,
And gently turned his form around;
And moving slowly on before,
She lead her lover toward the door.
Like some half sleeping, weary child,
The man obeyed her will so mild.
He followed on as in a dream,
Nor lingered, while she leading him,
Approached a couch within a room,
Where he had often slept before.
She kissed him when she closed the door,
A sweet good night, and blessed him there.

Soon Nahor's cottage home was still,
Save for the cricket's lonely trill;
But sleep would not close Wilda's eyes,
No matter how the maiden tries.
The imp of thought kept crowding in
With things which of the day had been,
Until the watch bird of the barn
Had blown the bugle of the morn,
Then fickle sleep with fingers light,
Closed down her lids with touches slight;

Kezia leads the laughing troop.

And Wilda slept until the sun,
With fiery lance, his day begun.
Then gently stepping to the floor,
She softly moved to Gether's door.
Her eager senses pleasures thrill
She whispered, "he is sleeping still."
Then to the duties of the day,
She hastened lightly on her way.
The morning meal she swift prepared,
While wondering how her lover fared.
She saw from Babel passing out,
People with chattels all about,
From Babel's tower to seed the world,
Like thistle down by breezes hurled,
Then thought of Gether, where should he,
With stammering tongue directed be?
Her father rose and greeted her,
Then seated him for converse near.
She soon of Gether told him all;
She told him of his tongue's enthrall,
And wondered in her awful grief,
If aught there was for his relief.
She pondered on her girlhood days—
Of all the joys of childish ways,
And blushed at thought of feelings pent,
When he with other maidens went.
She wondered if Kezia fair
Than she could better break the snare—
If love, the key of words and hearts,
Would turn if she should try her arts.
But where could now Kezia be?
Could she her lover send to see
One who might take her life away,
By taking him who had full sway
In her own heart, forever true,
Which had no room for lovers new.

She won the battle with a sigh—
She would to find Kezia try.

Her father called her to his side,
And said, "My dear, let faith abide
"For we will find, my child, a way
"To loose his tongue this very day.
"I know of one of Ancient Days,
"Who knows of man in all his ways.
"This ancient one, Melchizedek,
   The king of Salem we will seek.
"We will to him a journey take,
"My daughter, dear, for Gether's sake.
"He is the beauteous King of Love,
"Sufficient now his power will prove.
"He'll break the bonds which bind the boy,
"Who then will sing and shout for joy;
"And you, my child, shall join with him,
"And praise the king of fair Salem.
"This wondrous king to-day I hear,
"Will journey through the land of Ur.
"If you with horses ride to-day,
"You will to-morrow cross his way,
"For he from Niniveth has come,
"From visiting at Asshur's home.
"You need but tell your lover's plight,
"When he will gladly set it right.
"And by the setting of the sun
"To-morrow will the deed be done.
"For he our brother is, in love,
"And gladly will his goodness prove."

By this the morning meal was spread,
And Gether now had left his bed;
With dreamy step he moved about
Till Wilda came and led him out.

She seated him upon a chair.
With them their frugal meal to share,
And beamed with love while silently
The youth was quaffing at his tea.
It seemed to her an awful spell,
Which held her Gether's tongue so still,
So strange that not a loving word
Could he interpret though he heard.

The meal, of course, was ended soon,
Preparing for their trip begun.
Sweet Wilda dressed her all in gray,
To cleanly go the dusty way.
The carriage driven to the door,
Found her in waiting there before.
Then gently leading Gether forth
She turned their prancing chargers forth
Along Euphrates grassy slopes,
Toward the fruiting of her hopes,
Where Gether's tongue again set free,
And love implanted like a tree,
Within his soul to bloom and bear
The fruit of honest love for her.
He, like a little child, obeyed,
While seeming of himself afraid.
So Wilda held the tightened reins
Against the horses eager strains,
And while the river rolled away,
They rode in silence all the day.
At night they rested at an inn,
At morn another day begun.
The steeds more quiet paced along,
And Wilda's heart was filled with song.
Forgot the weary arms which held
The straining reins; her mind was filled
With hope for Gether, love restored,

As when a boy he chased the bird
Or butterfly, alone for her,
All done in young affection pure.
Forgetting greed and mighty names,
Forgot ambition's selfish aims;
With duty ever in his eye,
And all his hopes and aims on high.
With love his constant guiding star
And Wilda all his hopes to share.
She knew before the moon arose,
They sure would reach the town of Is,
Where on the morrow Salem's king
Should do for them a blessed thing.

They found the ancient village quite
Filled with excited stir that night,
For each would do his humble share,
While Salem's monarch lingered there.
To them it was a wondrous thing
To just behold the beauteous king.

Sleep was a bashful maid that night,
And touched our Wilda very light,
But Gether slept the hours away
Till opened wide the doors of day.
Melchizedek had crossed the stream,
While Gether lingered in a dream.
The town of Hit her farewell said,
While all the world was still in bed,
But Wilda fair, all dressed in white,
Was kissed by the departing night,
Before the sun rebuked the act
Or on the earth made his attack,
While fairer than the morning, she
Upon a porch where she could see
Watched for the coming of the king

Across the river, greatest thing
To happen in the town of Is.
Again for many, many days.
Her hair upon her shoulder fell,
Held to her temple by a shell,
The only ornament she wore,
It could not make her beauty more.
She trembled while she thought of he
That day her wondering eyes should see.
Her heart was filled with reverent awe,
While out across the stream she saw
The royal barge majestic glide,
And gracefully approach her side.
The changing blushes paint her cheeks,
As she her Gether quickly seeks.
She led him with a gentle hand,
Upon the porch with her to stand.
So there they stood that summer morn,
The day for Gether love was born,
And waited for the king to come,
To send them both rejoicing home.
At last he stood upon the shore,
No fairer person seen before:
His form of perfect mold and grand,
A palm of peace within his hand.
His locks and beard like raven's wing.
He such an one as poets sing.
In glances keen his piercing eye,
As blue as ever Eden's sky,
Beheld the maiden standing there.
Of all earth's creatures she most fair.
A look of love flowed o'er his face,
As with a step of stately grace
He moved toward the waiting pair,
Who would his holy blessing share.

"I know, my daughter, never fear.
"We will your lover's senses clear,
"His sweetest accents you shall hear.
"He upward turned his loving eyes,
"For benedictions from the skies:
"Oh, Father, from thy place on high,
"Behold us with thy loving eye.
"Plant from the garden up above
"Within our hearts the seed of love,"
Petitioned there the beauteous King,
For Gether's sake this holy thing.
A holy light o'erspread his face
Which filled with beauty all the place.
From Gether's bosom rolled a sigh,
A tear coursed downward from his eye;
His lythe young form in trembling stood,
His tongue spoke not the word he would.
Melchizedek uplifted then
His loving eyes to heaven again,
And pressed his hand on Gether's brow,
Who spoke and shouted glory now.

Sweet Wilda dropped her lover's hand
They both in reverent silence stand
Before the king whose wondrous power
Had brought to them this happy hour.
"Oh, Father," murmured Wilda low,
"Our life, our happiness must come
"From thee alone, while earth's our home.
"Our tongues alone can ne'er express
"How wonderfully thou dost bless."

"Aright, my daughter; true art thou,
"To give to God the glory now,"
The King replied with looks benign
Which o'er his noble features shine.
"Now, son," said he, "take Wilda's hand,

"And thus in holy presence stand.
"United now before the throne,
"Take Wilda for thy very own.
"She loves thee as her very life.
"Now take her here to be thy wife.
"Thy love which loosed thy tongue to-day
"Will with thee both forever stay."
  Then lifting heavenward his eyes,
  Asked God to make them good and wise.
  With hands upon their bowing heads,
  Petitioned for their earthly needs,
  And then, "before the throne," he said,
"My children thou are duly wed."
  Then turning from them he was gone,
  And left them standing there alone.
  Their hearts were filled with tender awe,
  As the retreating form they saw.
  They felt that they had surely then
  In presence more than angels been.
  Then Gether, with his own right arm,
  Gently encircled Wilda's form.
"My Wilda," softly whispered he,
"Words cannot speak my love for thee.
"My heart, my life, all, all are thine
"And naught on earth shall come between.
"Melchizedek has taught me love
"And I my life will spend to prove
"That God and thou art dear to me,
"And that my home in heaven shall be.
  A heavenly smile on Wilda's face
  Answered to Gether's fond embrace.
  He led her to the looking glass,
  That she might see e'er she should pass.
  And gazing there in mute surprise,
  A pearl gleamed soft before her eyes:
  The shell which fastened up her hair,

Contained a jewel rich and rare.
"Our blessings now should quite suffice
"We have the pearl of greatest price,"
Said Gether, as with gentle hands
He softly stroked the silken strands
Of Wilda's soft and flowing hair,
And kissed her rosy cheek so fair.

The journey home, a heavenly ride,
Along Euphrates flowing side,
A dream of bliss for groom and bride.
A father's blessing waited them,
When up to Nahor's door they came.
The skies were blue, the fields were green,
When this young pair their life began.
The years which pass, the years to come
Could find no sweeter happy home
In Shinar's fair and flowery land,
Than that controlled by Wilda's hand;
And always when they looked upon
Eventful days which now where run,
From Aryana's fields so fair
To mighty deeds in Shinar there,
Where Nimrod builded Babel's walls
Mid selfishness the heart appalls,
Confounding tongues that awful day,
The people scattered far away;
No scene or deed in retrospect
Upon which mortals could reflect
Was e'er so wondrous grand and great
As meeting with Melchizedek.

1776—THE ELOPEMENT—1897

(A Fourth of July Rhyme.)

Once on a time (for sure, there is no other way to start,
When to the friends all gathered round, you would a tale impart),
There was a handsome dame they called Britannia at court,
Her husband—well, if you don't mind, we'll call him John for short.

These people had a daughter fair, they called her Columbine;
You'd travel half the world around to find a maid so fine.
And still it was'nt strange at all that such a comely pair
In lawful, honest wedlock wed should have a child so rare.

Nor was it strange that beauty such as Columbina's was
Should have a swarm of lovers all around her form to buzz;
And so she had, but told them all, as gently as she could,
That she must love the man she took for evil or for good.

The folks looked on complacently, it pleased their parent pride
To see the gallant lovers press about their daughter's side.

But all this time the maiden grew, and soon she was
    of age,
And sometimes took her own sweet way despite her
    father's rage.

And John said to Britannia, "I fear the day will come
"We'll find it awful troublesome to keep the girl at
    "home."
And John was right, for sure enough, a lover did
    appear,
To whom their Columbina lent a very willing ear.

And then the wayward maiden, with her parents had
    a fuss,
Because she got their tea one day into an awful muss.
And while they stormed about the tea and did the
    girl berate,
She slipped out through the door and met her lover
    at the gate.

His name was Jonathan, and he was not a handsome
    lad,
But Columbina loved him with all the soul she had;
And so one day she told them that she and Jonathan
Would like to have their blessings e'er their wedded
    life began.

Then John he swore with all his might, Britannia
    she cried,
To think a plebian should win their daughter from
    their side.
And John roared "No!" That such a thing should
    never, never be;
If such a dolt as Jonathan should take her, he would
    see!

The lovers slipped away one day and slyly they were
    wed,
Though followed close by John and spouse through
    forest, field and mead.
At last the parents overtook the newly-wedded pair,
Where resting at a wayside inn complacently they
    were.

Then John sent word to Jonathan and Columbine to
    come,
For he and mother in their room would interview
    them some.
The young folks came, Britannia with tears her
    daughter hugged,
But John grew red and swelled with rage, and said
    he would be "chugged."

The young folks had been in the room a minute,
    maybe more,
When John got up and scowled at them and locked
    the parlor door.
And "now," said he to Jonathan, "you stole my
    "daughter, sir,
"And I shall beat you black and blue before from
    "here you stir."

John stormed about the room and swore, the women
    begged and wept,
While Jonathan, long, lank and cool his temper
    calmly kept.
And kept an eye on John, it seemed, for when John
    tried a crack
His son-in-law's right foot slid out and John lay on
    his back.

Now, John was stout and heavy, and thought that
    he could fix

If Jonathan he once could get his brawny arms be-
        twixt,
For Jonathan, while six feet three, was slim as any
        rake,
And John believed a good stout squeeze his limber
        back would break.

But, by some strange fatality, he never could just get
Quite close enough to hug the lad, before he'd be up-
        set.
And so it went a dozen times, till John was out of
        wind,
While Jonathan his long chin stroked and didn't
        seem to mind.

"I'm all knocked up. I didn't think a slender Yankee
        "lad
"With such a simple way could use a fellow up so
        "bad.
"And now, Britannia," said he, "we'll have to let
        "them go
"They'll have to run their own affairs; I'll never help
        "them to."

Upon their farm the young folks settled next to one
        of John's,
And there they prospered wonderfully, the story told
        me runs.
Till now the old folks think 'twould be a very proper
        thing
For two such prosperous farmers to join in laboring

Britannia, still a handsome dame, and buxom for her
        years,
And John, a portly gentleman, who always reason
        hears,

And side by side may Stars and Stripes and Union Jack
float high.

Believe, for keeping straight affairs, a union would
    be good,
And that they better could keep peace within the
    neigborhood.

So John and Jonathan now meet to talk of business
    things;
Britannia visits Columbine and with her sewing
    brings.
The old folks find that Jonathan is not so bad a chap,
And Columbine, with all her charms, could have done
    worse, mayhap.

Of course they have their differences, may be upon a
    race,
Or on a fence, or boundary somewhere about the
    place.
But nothing serious occurs to mar the common weal,
And no new wounds created which reason cannot
    heal.

And all the neighbors round about walk in a way
    correct;
They know that John and Jonathan insist upon re-
    spect.
They look with awe upon their wealth, their influence
    and power,
And say that no such farmer men were ever seen be-
    fore.

So let us hope that peace may last 'twixt John and
    Jonathan,
Until the sun and moon and stars have all their
    courses run,
And side by side may Stars and Stripes and Union
    Jack float high,
And may their waving, silken folds print "Justice"
    on the sky.

TRILLIUM.

Wakerobin, dressed in white and green,
    Came out on Easter day,
As fair a flower as e'er was seen
    By glade or woodland way.
Her bonnet white spread out upon
    Her robe of royal green,
Her amber throat rich nestling
    The wax-like leaves between.

We gather from among the moss
    This lovely Easter flower,
Which turns the brown of early spring
    Into a fairy bower.
She comes before the other blossoms
    Dare to face the blast,
To welcome back the birds who sing
    While gaily flitting past.

As spring grows old and roses bud,
    And summer days draw nigh,
She dons a purple bonnet,
    And with spring bids us good bye.
But wakerobin we'll ne'er forget
    While welcoming newer flowers,
For she it was, midst frosts of spring,
    Made glad this world of ours.

DUTY.

A duty done is worth a thousand dreams,
And nothing's mean, no matter how it seems,
That's set before us, and that we should do
To free ourselves and make the record true.

The smile of heaven is on little things;
The stories of our victories fly on angel's wings.
A thoughtful soul in some plain humble home
Makes of its deeds performed a mighty sum.

Rewards are not for what we dream to do,
But for the little things we see, and do them, too.
Time spent in dreams of mighty deeds
The Great Rewarder never even heeds.

The faithful ones are those who toil at home,
And do the little things that to them come;
Nor fear that others will not do their share,
But feel each duty as a favor rare.

He who shall hear the words "well done,
Thou good and faithful servant," from the Son,
Will be the one, the blessed Jesus says,
Who guards his steps in all the smallest ways.

THE MOTHERS' CONVENTION.

'Twas the "Mothers' Convention," assembled to see
What duties in households of mothers should be.
The most of the delegates gathered, believed
That many a mother was grossly deceived
By the idea that housekeepers' duties were plain,
And needed no speeches or essays to train.

To "clear up" such notions, it said in the call
This meeting would gather in Talkaby hall.
So we find them assembled, a company fair,
Each snapping with ideas and loaded for bear;
For old fashioned notions of what mothers were
Must be scrubbed away and the sky be made clear.

To the chair they elected a Miss Lemonbee.
"I never had any children," said she.
"But I know how they ought to be managed quite
    "well,
"For my sister has three," and forgot quite to tell
That she had helped spoil both the girl and the boys,
By denying them quite all their young childish joys.

The mothers then chose for their secretary
A widow who never had had round her play
A mischievous urchin or sly maiden mouse,
To muddy the carpet or brighten her house.
She, too, in her talk, thought she very well knew,
In all household affairs, what a mother should do.

The principal speaker, the mother of one
Spoiled monkey, imagined that under the sun
She could tell, if not do, with success what was right,

And of course was not bashful to speak with her might,
Of the theories she had evolved, while a nurse
Had the boy on the sidewalk or highway, of course.

They held their convention, and when they got through
They made up their minds what a wife "shouldn't do;"
And that was the principal thing they required;
Obedience wasn't a thing they admired,
Of duties the minimum number they'd know
And of children to bother their lives quite as few.

And so when mothers' convention adjourned
The mothers(?) as *wise as they went there returned.
To "appear" on the platform of course they had learned,
But children and household disdainfully spurned.
Forgetting the crown of obedience rare
Which patience shall place on a true mother's hair.

---

*Job xxviii. 28.

THE RULE OF CLOTH.

A man in denims blue or brown is just as much a man
As he arrayed in finest garb, to suit the tailor's plan.
But walking down the street alone, unless perchance, it be
Just previous to election day, his friends would never see.
If he should to a meeting go dressed in his working clothes,
He'd to a distant seat be shown, or ordered out, who knows?

A little child though fairer far than any playing round,
If dressed in garments cheap and plain would never hear the sound
Of words of praise, or feel, perchance, a single soft caress
From those who measure beauty out and sugar plums by dress.

A woman clothed in calico, though full of grace inate
Would freeze from icy glances of sisters dressed in state;
She easily could occupy a whole church pew alone,
For to the haughty dames about she'd surely not be known.

Now others over this might mope and shed some bitter tears,
But I pursue my quiet way, nor have poured in my ears

The sickening, drooling words of he whose scraping
    steps attend,
Like flies in sugar, wealth and dress, nor knows the
    name of friend.

TACOMA—RAINIER.

Tacoma-Rainier, mountain reigner,
That, true, is what you are,
The world admits, when it beholds you.
One name's enough for others,
But for you, not too many two.
Sublime, silent and grand you rear
Your hoary head above the bed
Where purest ether's born
From out the bowels of the virgin sea.

Mountain reigner, soverign king are you,
Others as vassals only serve
Among your mighty train.
Silent and rugged, too, are they
Their only duty there to somber stand
And by comparison your kingly form accentuate.
While you, crowned by the frost hosts,
Tacoma-Rainier, mountain reigner are,
Enthroned acknowledged sovereign
Over all your princely retinue.

A DREAM.

I traveled o'er a lonely road one dank November day,
And as the night drew on apace I hastened on my way;
For I must rest, I knew not where, in this vast wilderness,
No cabin in the gathering gloom did peering vision bless.
Now and again a glancing shot of rain upon my cheek
Warned me that I must hasten on, and needed shelter seek.

At last, among the dripping trees, a cottage I espied;
To its inviting window light I quickly turned aside.
I slept within this humble house, and as I sought my bed
I heard the rain drops pattering on the shingles overhead.

I stretched myself upon my couch and soon was fast asleep,
Oblivious of earthly things although the sky should weep.
And though on foot all day I'd toiled quite hard enough it seemed,
I kept right on with all my might a walking as I dreamed.

I stood, I dreamed, upon the shore by old Niagara,
And watched, amid the boom and roar the foaming waters play.
With awe and silence I beheld the mighty torrent's rush.

The air, and human gazers stood, filled with respectful hush.
And words were mean and man a mite amid the whelming sound;
The giant of the river's tread shook hard the frightened ground.

While wrapt with awe and gazing on the new and misty scene,
O'ercome with nature's mighty works, a curtain fell between,
And I awoke and knew the truth, by listening aloof,
For now the rain poured down in sheets upon my bedroom roof.
And this with wind among the trees was my Niagara.
Sadly I turned upon my couch and slept till break of day.

TRYING TO FORGET.

Oh, those little feet, how quickly all about the place they'd go,
From the kitchen to the chamber and the cellar down below;
To the barn, and to the orchard, to the milk house and the spring,
For our daughter, aged four, must have a hand in everything.

If the day was set for baking she was surely making bread,
If the churning was made ready, she'd become a dairy maid.
If old Ginger horse was harnessed and was taken from his stall,
It must surely be to give a ride to Eva and her doll.

But one day they took our darling to the city on the hill,
Where the streets are sad and solemn and the houses always still,
Where the inmates never answer to the low and pleading cry
At the doorway of their dwellings, where they ever silent lie.

They cleared away the baby's things while we were gone that day,
To kindly help us to forget, in such a simple way.
But when we came back to the house it was so lone and still
That nothing came into our thoughts but Eva on the hill.

Then at evening, in the gloaming, in the "now I lay
 me" time,
To sustain us in our awful grief required support from
 Him.
When we missed the little cradle sitting close beside
 our bed,
Which so long had pillowed sweetly angel face and
 fluffy head.

While the baking and the churning and the milking
 must be done,
Just the same as when our darling came to help at
 every one.
The little loaves were missing, and the bitter tears
 would drop,
And I mourned, while milking Mooley, for the little
 waiting cup.

But the thing which broke me up the most, when I
 was all alone,
And getting out old Ginger when a lonely week had
 gone,
Was a little ragged dolly, down by the manger side,
Where our baby girl had dropped it when last she
 took a ride.

Oh, that yellow-headed dolly, which her little hands
 had held,
How it flowed my cup of sorrow already more than
 filled.
As tenderly I gathered up the soiled and tattered
 thing
It seemed that I must almost hear the merry laughter
 ring.

But the weary days have lengthened into slowly moving years,

Hopes for future joys and brightness take the place of 'gretful tears,
And the summer land of gladness with our baby 'mid the flowers
With its peaceful rippling waters we believe will soon be ours.

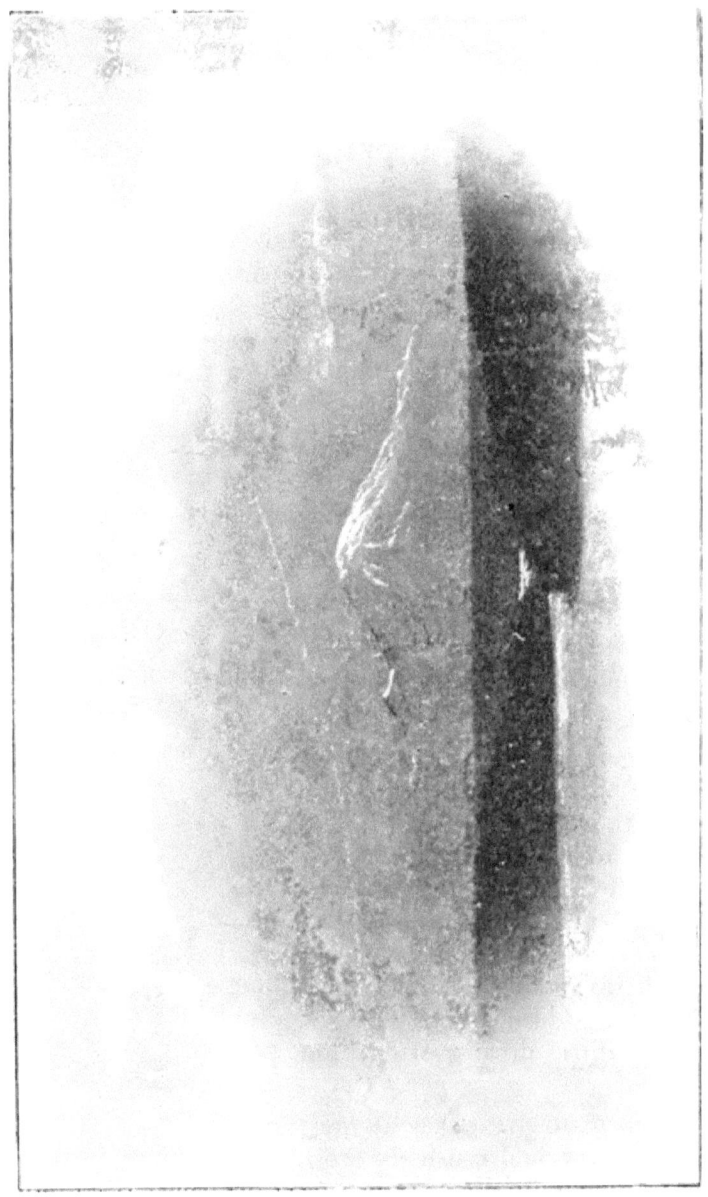

Goliath Great among the hosts.
Supreme he rules nor needs to boast.

THE MOUNTAIN.

The mighty mountain of the Sound
Looked down upon the forest round.
Solemn and still, a guard he stood,
Between Columbia's mighty flood
And Frazer's winding, golden stream,
The farmer's home, the miner's dream.

His whitened locks blow in the wind,
And with the blue of Heaven blend.
He stands, with nothing round to hide,
His tall fir bayonets beside,
And frowning, looks upon the world,
His only rival, flags unfurled,
Who with noisy, hoyden day,
Will sport the fleeting hours away.

He stands mid mountain troop around,
Upon them calmly looking down.
Goliath great among the host,
Supreme he rules, nor needs to boast,
For all can see, with wondering eyes,
The silent mountain pierce the skies—
Can see his pale and silent face,
With frown look down from endless space,
As though in meditation deep,
Or wrapt in dreams of daylight sleep.

His form so great that he must know
To move would crush the world below;
For though austere, and boding harm,
His heart within is throbbing warm.

With silent care he broodeth o'er
The sleeping world along the shore;
He stands above with brow so white,
The sentinel of sombre night.

With busy day he saw begin
The toils of men with strife and din;
The cities on the winding Sound,
Among the forest scattered round;
With eager blush the guiling dawn,
The world from silent slumber drawn.

He saw the world with twilight part;
Their kisses seemed to touch his heart.
Across his austere visage came
A rosy blush, but not of shame,
For well he knew the bitterness
Which made their loving pleasures less,
The sorrow which within them passed
That their sweet meeting could not last;
That sombre night must separate
The lovers e'er the hour grew late.

And so we love our mountain grand,
The noblest in all the land,
Who towers beside the western sea,
Where all the passing world may see;
Who always at his post is found,
The sentinel of Puget Sound.

*BY CHANCE.

Luke x. 31.

By chance? By chance? A chance for what?
A chance for kind and loving thought;
A chance to bind our neighbor's bruise;
A chance our Savior's gifts to use;
A chance to do, a chance to love,
A chance the Spirit's power to prove.

What is the chance which rules with aught
That is to us with import fraught?
The chance to give the cooling cup;
The chance to lift our brother up;
The chance by love and kindly act
To prove that we are God's in fact.

All have a chance to see the light;
God's Spirit pierces sin's dark night,
And gives a chance to look and live;
A chance to trust, a chance to give;
A chance to work, a chance to grow;
A chance for glory here below.

The priest chanced, then, to pass that way,
God did not chance to test that day,
But gave him there a chance to do
A work to make the record true,
Which should be read "well done," if he
Should not fall short, and duty see.

---

*Written while Rev. T. J. Massey was preaching a sermon on this text in Blaine, Wash., March 8, 1896.

So we've a chance, both great and small,
A chance (the greatest gift of all)
By faith the sons of God to be,
To help the world his glory see.
Then may we thank him day by day
For chances sent by him our way;
For tests to prove us, though e'er hard,
Which fit us for His great reward.

SLEEP.

Thou strange twin sister unto quiet death,
And just as fair, but for disturbing breath,
Why should not two such witching creatures rare
A single personal existence share?

Why should you at the break of dawning day
Your robe of sweet oblivion drop away?
Why should your lovely sister, hovering near,
At sunrise so mysteriously disappear?

Thou canst not tell us, we shall never know,
Until by thee from mortal realms we go,
And clearly see amid the courts above,
Behind the curtain raised by hands of love.

Where the wind among the balsam boughs celestial music makes.

PICTURES.

It is evening in the homestead, and the gleams of twi-
    light go,
While the rocking chair swings slowly in the firelight
    to and fro;
And I listen, while I'm dreaming, to the crooning
    lullaby
      Of a mother with her baby in her arms.

It is evening in the forest, and the camping pioneer
Is walled about by shadows, dancing silently and
    queer,
And beside the campfire watching, while the embers
    fade and fall,
      Sits a mother with her baby in her arms.

It is evening on the desert, and the famished travelers,
While they totter 'mid the burnings, have to drink but
    dew of tears.
When they fall, as fall the shadows, never more to rise
    again,
      There's the mother with her baby in her arms.

It is evening on the ocean, and about a little boat
The briny billows glisten and the brassy heavens gloat.
Thirst and hunger gaunt and horrid, seizing on their
    helpless prey,
      Take a mother with her baby in her arms.

It is evening in the arctic, and the earth is buried deep
In its shroud of winter whiteness, there to rest in icy
    sleep;

Hovering like a marble statue, where the campfire's
    glow has died,
  Sits a mother with her baby in her arms.

It is evening in the ruins where relentless fire has
    swept,
Where upon the dreams of childhood cruel flames
    have softly crept;
There among the smouldering embers where have
    tripped the busy feet
  Lies a mother with her baby in her arms.

It is evening in the valley, and the floods are out in
    glee,
Grasping in their cold embraces forms which cannot
    up and flee;
They have tossed with cruel wanton on the grasses by
    the shore
  A mother with her baby in her arms.

It is evening time in heaven, and the glowing sunlight
    streams
Down upon the walls of jasper, in its softest golden
    gleams,
And it rests in glorious halo, just before the pearly
    gate,
  On a mother with her baby in her arms.

MY BROKEN FLOWER.

My sweetest flower was broken when it came to me;
My heart was sore and sad, I could not see why this
    should be.
I gazed upon its broken little stalk
And wondered why 'twas so my hopes to mock,
And then I gazed again, and lo! beheld
A something which my hungry bosom swelled,
For in my broken flower I saw a smile
Which could not but my tearful heart beguile;
Like Lea, "tender-eyed," it looked at me,
        My broken flower.

While gazing on my broken little flower
There came to me sweet solace for the hour.
For in its smiling, upturned face I saw
Pictures such as only angels draw.
In colors, changing deep and heavenly rare,
Like flowers of Paradise and soft as maiden's hair.
I thanked the Gardener who gave it then;
It in my garden grew where sorrow'd been;
And there with love my eager steps I bend
With quiet peace my broken flower to tend,
        My broken flower.

MY LITTLE GIRLS.

I am sitting here this golden day,
With no little girls around me at play
    The house is so still,
    I can hear the trill
    Of the bobolink below the hill in the meadow
        far away.

No curling heads or bright blue eyes,
Nor little voices with questions wise
    Crowd round my knee
    As they used to be
    When I listened to my little girls three, to what
        each should surmise.

No dollies now or playthings about,
Or little feet running in and out.
    Their playhouse is near,
    But with no girlies here,
    Nothing in all the earth can cheer like my little
        ones' merry shout.

Oh where, oh where are my little girls gone,
Who used to run when my work was done
    From the garden gate,
    Where they'd been to wait
    For papa, who, though a little late, was never
        too tired for fun?

They are gone, those three little girls of mine,
To the land of womanhood lang syne;
    And alone, to-day,
    How I miss their play,
    And the hours forever gone away, to ne'er return however I pine.

CHINOOK.

'Twas our first year's abode in the Evergreen State,
And the summer to us seemed to linger quite late,
But October had come with its clouds and its rain;
The forest had carpets of fallen leaves lain;
Jack Frost but few visits had made to the Sound,
'Twas vain that we looked for old winter around.

In November both summer and autumn played free,
While the cattle smiled broadly the green grass to see;
Old winter kept out, and with trembling shook,
As he saw the bright sun, and felt gentle Chinook.

December came on with its gay Christmas week,
And still were no storms with frost cold and bleak,
But the roses bloomed gaily and smiled at the sun,
And the pansies nod chipperly every one.
The primrose and vinca were out at their best,
All looking quite gay in their new autumn dress.

A cloud came along while they stood in a row
And covered them up with a blanket of snow,
But the gentle Chinook, the very next day,
With a tender reproof pulled the blanket away.

And so flew the time, until glad new year's day
For a week to the bygone had passed in its way.
The wind roared louder and drifted the rain,
Still we wondered if we would have winter again.
While the gales whistled hard from the south, west
    and east,
The gentle Chinook still pled softly for peace.

But there came a sad day when Boreas' young son,
A dissolute youth, who cared for but fun,
Ranged around through the mountain with wild wanton look,
And in his brass boldness cared not for Chinook;
So he turned loose a blast lade with snow and with frost,
Till poor little Chinook in the blizzard was lost;
And the wild winds came down with a whistle and tear
From the cold northeast where the green glaciers are.

Cold winter was here and we sat round the fire,
Piling pitchwood and fir knots up higher and higher;
And wished, if we ventured the threshold to pass,
For rain and not frost, but for flowers and grass.

We longed for the breath of the gentle Chinook
To tinge the cold sky with a softening look.
A fortnight we mourned for the musical breeze,
Which should come from the south and sing in the trees.

We waited and watched till the time seemed so long,
We never should hear that sweet soul-melting song;
But gentleness won in the contest at last,
And Chinook came along on a south wind that passed.
She spoke to the earth and it softened his heart,
Sent back to the mountains the cold with a start.
The buds on the trees swelled with gladness to see,
And the flowers guaranteed that she welcomed should be.
She brought back the birds in the second month soft,
Whose heart she had melted completely and oft.
So winter was over, praise God for the look,
Of gentle, soft-spoken, life-giving Chinook.

Oh, the Golden Gate is far away on the shores of California.

THE GOLDEN GATE.

"Where is the Golden Gate, Mamma?"
Asked little Jane, in tones of awe.
"Is there a really truly gate,
"Like ours, where we all go to wait
"For Papa, when he's been at work,
"And then come home before it's dark?"

"The Golden Gate," said Mamma, "is where
"Saint Peter waits at the top of the stair,
"And welcomes in the true and good
"(Who have done on earth just as they should)
"To the glad green fields of Paradise,
"Where everything is pure and nice."

"Oh, yes, I know," said the little one,
"That's away in Heaven above the sun,
"But isn't there one somewhere more near,
"And not so far away from here?
"It seems to me that Sisiter Kate
"Told the other day of a golden gate
"Where people live in a big, big town,
"At a place where they say the sun goes down.
"And where there are ships and mountains, too,
"A city of houses, really and true.

Said Mamma, "you dear old fashioned child,"
While she kissed the little maid and smiled:
"There is a Golden Gate, my dear,
"Where the skies are soft all through the year;
"Where the rivers and sea played basket ball
"In the rocks and sand and broke the wall,

"And piled the rocks and sand aside
"And were helped in their work by the wind and tide.
"They made a gate for the singing sea
"To come inside in gladsome glee
"And play with the rivers twice each day
"At the place where the ocean lions stay.

"The Spanish gallions passing by,
"Sailed far away under southern sky,
"In a mad, mad search for glittering spoil,
"The fruits of others' weary toil.
"They scanned the shores of the Golden State,
"But missed in their search its big front gate.

"But where is the Golden Gate?" again
 In eager accents queried Jane.

"Oh, the Golden Gate is far away,
"On the shores of California,
"Where the poppies shine like yellow suns,
"Upon the flowery summer dunes;
"And where the palm and orange trees
"Drop sweet perfumes upon the breeze,
"And the blood of the luscious grape is shed,
"In a flowing stream of rich, rich red.

"But how about the gate, Mamma?
"Do tell me, please, and right away."

"Oh, the Golden Gate you could not climb
"To await Papa at evening time,
"Nor could you swing, when it opened wide,
"Upon the top of its flowing tide.
"The gate is not of gold, my dear,
"But the sands of the flowing rivers were,
 "And so they called it the Golden Gate,

"For it leads to the gold of the Golden State.
"And when the sun sets in the sea,
"And his face looks through where the gate should be
"The waves with a splendor glow untold
"In the sunset like a sea of gold;
"And the place is always open wide,
"For the gliding ships on the glowing tide,
"And this, my dear, is the magic gate
"Which leads to the fields of the Golden State."

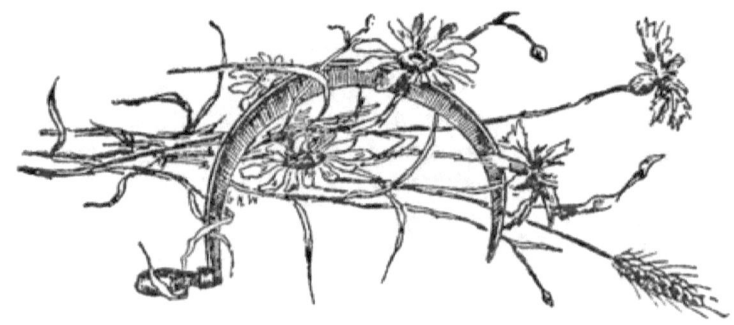

THE CRASH ON THE L. & B.

You say I am finished, doctor,
  And you'd save me if you could?
Well, I don't know but it's just as well,
  For I never was much good.
What can you do for me?
  And what word would I like to leave?
Just ease my shoulder a little,
  And pull away that sleeve.

Now, in my side pocket there,
  If it hasn't been spilled and lost
You will find in a little leather book,
  A letter that you may post.
Yes, that's it, its directed to her,
  You will send it, doc., all right,
Oh, thank you, you are very kind,
  She'll get it to-morrow night.

It's worth five thousand dollars, doc.,
  That letter is, to her,
If I die, as you say, before sundown,
  It hurts me here to stir.
I fixed it up this morning, doc.,
  Before I took the train
And doctor, a drop of water, please,
  Oh, that was an awful pain.

I didn't know but I might get hurt
  But didn't expect quite this,
But when we tumbled down that bank
  'Twould be strange if I should miss,

And come from this pile of kindling wood
    Alive to tell of it,
With the train all smashed in such a way
    Oh, hadn't I better sit?

I've been looking for weeks for a place to work
    And make a living in,
But I haven't more than made my way
    Wherever I have been;
So I thought I'd go to the city and see
    What the chances were for me,
I didn't know that the thing would end
    In a ditch by the L. & B.

I had a letter from wife last week
    It was loving and kind and true,
But I wouldn't see her very soon
    When I read that letter, I knew.
"When you send me one hundred dollars
    "You have earned, not borrowed, see?
"I will start the next month to the end of the earth
    "To join you," she wrote to me.

Well, she'll get the hundred dollars all right,
    But won't need to follow me.
It must be getting dark, doc.,
    For its hard for me to see.
What, the sun is shining bright yet?
    And not a cloud in the sky,
Where are you? I cannot see you;
    There is something in my eye.

There, that will do, be easy now,
    And let me lie just so,
Unbutton my collar and let me breathe
    A little before you go.

She'll come to me after awhile, may be.
  I believe it's getting bright.
I thought of her and the babies last;
  Tell her, doc., good night.

THE LOST PICTURE.

Oh, Marguerite, who could have done it?
That bit of pasteboard with your shadow on it.
  They have taken it and left to me
  No token that the world can see.

But in the gallery of my aching heart
There hangs a picture which shall never part;
'Twas painted with the brush of glowing youth,
Exquisite bears the touch of lovely truth,
There it shall hang, draped in the lace of love,
The ideal of my youth, drawn from above,
Until the webs of doubt are brushed away,
In the glad dawning of the glory day.

FLOATING WITH THE STREAM.

Oft in the golden days of youth,
   When life was but a summer dream,
I've wandered off to some secluded nook
And idly watched the fleecy clouds,
   While gently floating down life's drowsy stream.

Unseen, unheard, the strife and toil,
   Left in the busy world behind,
While I with lazy longings lay and dreamed
Of joys unknown and sights unseen
   Which came unsought, which I shall never find.

That pleasure, oh, much sweeter far
   Than any worldly thing to be attained;
Nothing so fair as the kaleidoscope
Of boyhood's idle summer dreams,
   If to the bottom pleasure even drained.

Nothing on earth so really fair
   As seen through meshes of my old straw hat,
While I lay idly dreaming wide awake
Nor thought nor cared for aught,
   And no, not even thought of that.

But soon the boyhood dreams are past,
   The days to lie and idly dream,
And we, while mingling with the world,
With struggling strife of men,
   Are pulling hard against the flowing stream.

Yet, while we mingle in the struggle here,
   Still we may fix our gaze on things above,
And brighten up the strife and turmoil
Here below with mellow sunshine
   Through the gilding mesh of love.

BABY.

Oh, I know I can't describe her so that you can understand;
She not only is the sweetest child in all this mighty land,
But the whole world don't contain one half so nice as our Maree;
She's the softest, tenderest, sweetest one that ever you did see.
She's four months old, and laughs and crows and tries to talk and sing;
Her helpless moves are our delight, the cunning little thing.

I can't describe the look of satisfaction on her face,
As nestling on her mother's breast, her own especial place,
She croones and sighs contentedly and shuts her little eye,
And draws the living stream of life from baby's sweet supply.
If I could spell her goos and coos and all the things she says,
I'm sure 'twould make the biggest book I've seen in all my days,
But no matter how she twitters, "mamma's darling little bird,"
No one can understand at all a single blessed word.

The little hands go wandering, like a butterfly at play,
Never seeming to be guided in any certain way,
But like him, the little fist will find the very choicest place,

And settle down content upon the rosebud on her face.

Her little feet are moving back and forth both day and night;
Some one is sure to kiss them whenever they're in sight.
Her mamma holds them up to view full twenty times a day,
And says "they're sweet enough to kiss, now aint they, papa, say?"

She's not all soft, the little thing, for down her back's a bone;
Up goes her head, up go her feet, she'll try to sit alone.
She thinks if she should try enough she surely would be able
To straighten up her back and sit with mamma at the table.
She bobs and grunts and twists her face, puts up her head and feet;
She beats the air with little hands then gives it up complete.
You wouldn't think, to read these lines, that she is number ten,
But so it is, and still we think as nice as ever seen.
It may be so, as grandma says, the last is best of all;
She is, at any rate we think, the nicest one this fall.

POLITICS.

There is a sewer wide and deep which rolls its sluggish stream
Among the denizens of earth where countless millions teem;
Its stenchfull tide is turbulent with garbage dead and foul,
And on it microbes, revelling, are feeding cheek by jowl.

These microbes are a crafty crew, and each with schemes is big,
As squirming at their stenchfull feast they in the garbage dig,
And as they stench for stench oppose and burrow day by day
They think, to win the fight of life, there is no other way.

This sewer flows through all the world where striving mortals are,
They think the fumes of its ferment a needed evil are;
And so the creatures that it breeds increase from day to day,
And fatten on its reeking tide while in its depths they play.

These creatures are not vile entire, for some there are who dream
To eat away the growing filth, and purify the stream;
And some there are who fatter grow and bigger than the rest,

As squirming o'er their struggling mates they seek
   the reeking crest,
And chuckle while they trample down the weaker
   mites below
They think upon these simple ones, how little that
   they know.

Thus, "cursed is the man who trusts upon the arm of
   flesh,"
And thinks to overcome the vile by puny human wish.
And thus the putrid stream will flow while mortal
   man is blind,
Until with willing hearts and meek the source of truth
   they find,
Then, when by faith vain striving man obedience has
   learned,
This sewer will be closed for aye; its garbage will
   be burned.

THE STAR OF BETHLEHEM.

To the Christian Endeavor Convention,
San Francisco, July, 1897.

Over rivers, plains and mountains,
  With the bright star guiding them,
Came to the ancient Chaldees hastening
  To the rock of Bethlehem.

Guided by the power of *wisdom,
  Meek they sought that manger bed,
Where the **love of heaven was cradled,
  And its beams of glory shed.

Gifts they brought and sweet frankincense,
  Worshiped they the Prince of Peace,
While the angels o'er the shepherds
  Sang in strains which never cease.

Peace on earth, good will to all men,
  Was the song the angels sung,
And through ages down from Bethlehem
  Has the carroll ever rung.

Still the star is shining, shining,
  Lighting all to Jesus' feet;
Still the angels whisper carols,
  Everywhere God's children meet.

Over rivers, plains and mountains,
  With an aim both good and great,

---

*Job xxviii. 28.
**I. John iv. 8, 16; John x. 30.

Army of Christian Endeavour,
  To the sunset Golden Gate
Came, their footsteps hither guiding
  By the star of Bethlehem;
Here the love of heaven lingered,
  With his power o'erflowing them.

Here each soul in sweet communion,
  Filled with Christian sympathy,
Each becomes in each enfolded,
  With the moments passing by.

Shall the loving ties be broken
  Which have bound us here once more?
Never, they shall onward draw us
  Till we reach the Golden Shore.

And with loving eye all-seeing
  He will watch 'tween you and me,
While we're absent from each other,
  Until we his glory see.

THE DESERTED HOMESTEAD.

I've been to the old place to-day,
  Where we lived so many years;
Where we laughed our merriest laughter,
  And shed our bitterest tears.

I wandered out among the weeds,
  Where we planted in the spring,
And gathered in the autumn
  Increase from everything.

I sat in your old chair, wife—
  The one you loved the best—
In which, when tired at evening,
  You used to sit and rest.

The spring is covered o'er with weeds,
  I could not get a drink,
But sat me down upon the bank
  Beside it there to think.

The path, down which the children trooped
  To meet me when I came,
Is hid 'neath drooping grasses wet
  And does not look the same.

The birds and mice have taken charge
  Of the old house and shed,
And nothing but the legs and slats
  Are left of the high bed.

The old long cedar table,
  Round which we used to meet,

Is covered o'er with moss and dust,
   And nothing there to eat.

The chairs all lonely sit arow
   Along the old log walls;
Upon their homemade backs and seats
   Askance a sunbeam falls.

The cradle sits beside the door,
   A frock hangs on its rail,
But let me listen e'er so hard,
   I cannot hear a wail.

The orchard grows among the weeds,
   With briar and bramble filled,
And birds and rabbits roam about
   The grounds we often tilled.

The old home place calls up the years
   Of toil and hope gone by,
When prospects of the coming day
   Encouraged you and I.

The lake in quiet beauty lies,
   Among the forest green,
Just as it did in those old days,
   When we came on the scene.

A few more dwellings round it sit,
   And mirror in its face;
The waters sparkle just as bright,
   And you would know the place.

But turn away I must, and move
   Among the rushing throng;

Such quiet scenes and memories
  They cannot keep me long.

Good bye, old place, I'll come again
  And drink your quiet in,
And breathe your restful solitude,
  Where comes no turmoil in.

*MT. ST. ELIAS.

Gray peak of the north, majestic ye stand,
Silent, alone in your solitude grand.
Mount St. Elias, Father of Gold,
A guard to the glittering path to the cold.

    Your fires have died
      And your rocks are cold,
    But your veins are asparkle
      With glittering gold.
    Your fingers reach out
      To the north and the south
    To touch as with magic
      The aged and the youth.

    Your yellow veins flow
      From the fields of the sun;
    Through the hills
      Of the New El'd Orado they run,
    But the heart which supplies them
      Is hid in your breast,
    Whence the arteries flow
      To the east and the west.

Nature's crucibles melted your coffers to fill
With treasures you lavish the world at your will.
You stand by the path to the realms of cold—
Mt. St. Elias, Father of Gold.

---

*Written and published in 1888.

RIDING THE COLTS.

Looking backward through the years
With their mingling hopes and fears,
Through the vistas stretched away,
Still it seems but yesterday;
And the sight comes up as then,
With its merriment again.

How the shouts and laughter ring
As they go a-galloping,
Colts and boys and dog away,
On that bright and happy day.
I can see them now as then,
And it warms my heart again.

Colts are gone to horse-hereafter,
Boys are scattered, and their laughter
Only comes in memory,
As my heart looks back to see;
But the scene is cheering still,
Turn as often as I will.

Never brighter colts or boys
Joined in making frisky noise;
And the dog, of course, must be
One of such a party, he,
As they clatter in the ride
Out across the prairie wide.

How they ride, those boys of mine!
What care they for saddles fine?
Barebacked colts, barefooted boys,
Each seems to enter in the joys,

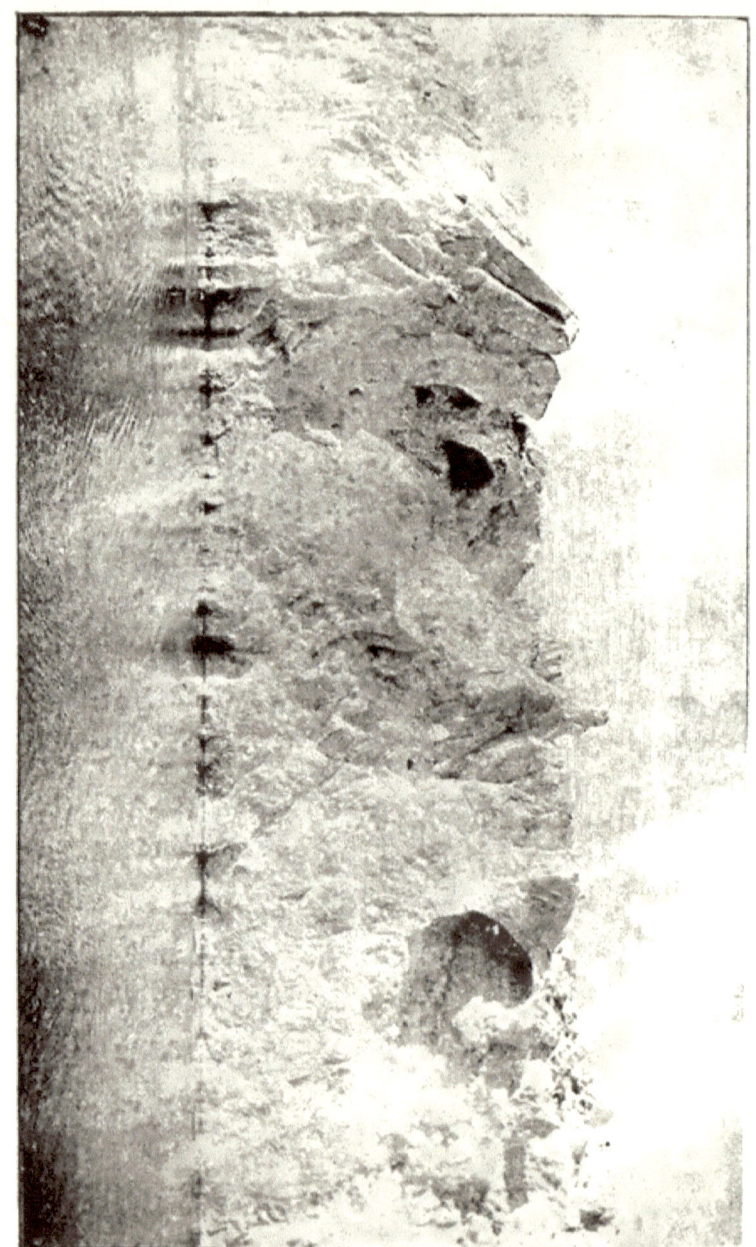

Muir Glacier, Alaska.

As out they troop across the plain,
A shouting, frisking, jolly train.

Which most playful are to-day—
Colts or boys—'tis hard to say.
Flora, mother of the herd,
Gets coltish when she hears the word,
Forgets her years and joins the race;
For her no youngster sets the pace.

And so they go across the plain,
With streaming tails and flowing mane.
Bold Morgan-Durock colts are they,
And out with boys and dog at play.
A ride for them is only fun—
Enjoyed as much as pasture run.

Ah, me, since then I've often seen
Many a charger sleek and clean,
But nothing like the woolly steeds
That galloped out across the meads,
Bestridden by four freckled boys,
Bent on fun and frisking joys.

No equipage, howe'er so fine,
Can I within my heart enshrine
Like that glad train of farmer's boys,
With dogs and colts and all their noise.
Those lusty colts—more beauteous steeds
Than e'er bestrode for val'rous deeds.

And as I think upon the past
I see them madly gallop fast
Away into the distant years.
I say, as gently fall the tears,
As Father Time the distance bolts:
"My boys come back and ride the colts."

THE BACHELOR.

In the past three years in the forests of Western Washington, in one county, the writer has known one young man who, while felling a tree, was crushed to death by a falling branch, and one who was shot and robbed in his cabin; one who was crushed and burned to death in his cabin; one who was drowned in the river close by his own door, and the following lines were written just after the burned remains of a fine young man from Iowa were discovered in the ruins of his cabin where he had died alone, leaving loving friends back in the Mississippi Valley to mourn the loss of their brave manly boy who was struggling to carve out a home in the forests:

Back in the woods in his cabin alone
With nothing to cheer when his day's work is done.
Save the rosy red firelight which glows in his eye,
Or his own teeming thoughts which give birth to a sigh—
His hopes, which are many, his books, which are few,
Or perchance his dog, who ever proves true.
An Adonis in beauty, Apollos in strength,
Is the sum when we dwell on his physique at length.
Alone in the woods with his axe and his thoughts
And no fortune but hope and a long row of naughts.

What does he here in this lone solitude,
With no sound but his echoing axe in the wood,
Or his own song or whistle sent back from the hills,
Which echo his soul with its loneliness fills.
Of what are his dreams as he sits by the fire.
His hands slowly ruffling his curly brown hair,
For to-morrow what hopes o'er his fancy now roll,

What picture is framed in the glass of his soul?
The smile rippling softly across his broad brow
Comes out from the scenes of his solitude now.

He's alone in the woods but his mind is away
For a taste of sweet joy where loving ones stay,
For a glimpse in the eye of she who he'd wife,
Or fond look at the woman who gave him to life.
Away with the ones who are dreaming at home
Of the day when their pride shall invite them to come.
He is thinking of them and his face is o'erspread
With a soft look of hope as he bows down his head,
And asks the great giver of good in the skies
To watch over all and keep tears from their eyes.

But he turns from his thoughts to his bachelor fare,
Which consists of no pastry or dainty bits rare;
He chokes as he swallows his desolate meal
With a cloy only those in forced hermitage feel.
He thinks of the toil and the struggles ahead—
Of the years before then, then goes weary to bed,
But awakes on the morrow with nothing but hope,
Only thoughts of the end and no time to mope.
He sees the good farm and the cottage he'll rear
And the sweet maiden there who the place will endear.
Each thought of this time in the futures so bright
Makes his heart and his axe and his labor grow light.

But hark! there's a lull in the crashing of trees,
And a low groan of agony glides o'er the breeze.
God grant that someone may be wandering near,
And this weak moan of sorrow may fall on his ear.
One shivering sigh and then all is still
Save the woodpecker perched in the tree on the hill.

Oh, angels look down from your heaven and weep
On the mother, the maiden, who smile in their sleep.
As they dream of the lad with the ringlets of brown
Who is toiling so bravely for love and his own.

Oh, weary the maiden grows counting the days,
How anxious the mother as sadly she prays.
No tidings from Fred as the months grow from weeks,
No peace for each fond one wherever she seeks,
At last, when poor nature had borne all it could
Came simply the message, "Found dead in the "wood."
"Oh, my boy!" moaned the mother, "thus lonely to "die—
"None to smooth the rough way or to close the bright "eye."
"Oh God!" mourned the maiden and clutched at her breast
As she prayed, "May my soul soon with him be at "rest."

They found him one day with a tree on his thighs
With one arm 'neath his head and the tears in his eyes.
By his side lay his axe, on its handle a name—
"Eloise," in deep letters, speaking love and its dream.
He had died with the crash which had pinioned him there;
Death had come without call or an agonized prayer.
And the brave lad they buried that day in the mold
Had the hopes of two women down there in the cold.
Then weep for the sorrow of mother and lass,
For the boy they both loved is now under the grass.

Back in the woods in his cabin alone,
The bachelor sits when his day's work is done;

Let no one speak lightly or smile at his lot,
For a hero is he who this battle has fought.
He may die in the crash of a tree o'er his head,
Or live to be burned in the wreck of his bed.
If madness should miss him in search for its prey,
The robber and murderer may cut short his day.
And the ashes his cabin has left on the ground
Tells not of the blood which is spattered around.
Thus oft' of our hermit, his pains and his groans
There is naught left to tell but a bundle of bones.

Seattle, 1889.

THE ALL NIGHT MEETING.

They'd been praying in the mission for the fire of Pentacost—
That with favor from the throne of grace the people might be blessed.
And that each and every soul might be filled up with holy fire.
That each one might be fed on food that should with life inspire.

They had their reg'lar meetings, and their day of fast and prayer
Right along, and an outsider would have said they had their share
Of the Spirit, and of blessings which were thrown in on the side,
But strange enough as it may seem they were not quite satisfied.

So they talked the matter over, Brother Work and Brother Good.
With the others they consulted to determine how they stood.
And when they'd prayed and fasted and hunted in the light
They agreed they'd hold a meeting that should last throughout the night.

So they gathered Sunday evening at the mission, reinforced
By a grave determination to combat with fire the worst.

There were songs and testimonies, prayers and speeches all about.
Everybody seemed delighted when good Brother True came out.
But a thing that marred the meeting, and it really was too bad,
Was chipping in by Brother Speake when anything was said.

However, things went well enough till twelve o'clock at night,
Until the people bowed themselves to try and get set right,
Then just as they were kneeling round and praying on the floor,
The lamp fell down on Sister True and made a fearful roar.

Then Brother Work, who heard the crash, but didn't look about,
Said "Praise the Lord!" with all his might in a triumphant shout.
But in a moment everyone knew what the trouble was,
And hurried round to fight the fire or sidle from the place.

But Brother Work came rushing up and piled the cushions on.
"I've fought the Devil oft' before," said he as he begun.
Soon, very soon the fire was out, the people, too, as well,
But then they gathered in again, their joys and fears to tell.

The next thing which disturbed the peace was when old Brother Speake
On baptism raised up his voice to a soprano shriek.
They couldn't sing or pray him down, but raised an awful din,
Till a poor drunkard passing asked, "Do I pay to get "in?"

At last old Brother Speake got up and took himself away,
Then Sister Bright said "praise the Lord, now let's "begin to pray."
Then Brother Boys went hand in hand along with Brother Good,
And singing walked about the room like "Children "in the Wood."
And everybody laughed in spite of all that they could do,
Until the tears ran down their cheeks, and sides were aching, too.

And then they each one told their faults, and testimonies flowed,
And prayers and songs and shaking hands until the roosters crowed.

At half-past six the meeting closed and all the folks went home,
And all agreed, or nearly all, that it had helped them some,
But still, an all-night meeting couldn't make the people love,
Unless they had a speaking tube connected up above,
And used it, too, quite frequently in meetings and outside,
And lived a life of righteousness, with nothing they would hide.

Oh, come where the stream of Oregon from the mighty mountain flows.

THE STREAM OF OREGON.

I am resting, sweetly resting, on the placid sea of years,
Where are no distressful longings and we shed no bitter tears;
In my rose-embowered cottage, while the time is gliding on,
In the shadow of the mountains by the stream of Oregon.

In the sunshine of the springtime when the soft chinook has come,
And the silent woods are gleaming with the waxen trilleum,
And the looms of nature's weavers have their carpeting begun,
I am glad I am a dweller by the stream of Oregon.

When the bowing fairy lily flecks the meadow o'er with white,
And the air so soft and balmy fills my spirit with delight,
Like the lambs within the pasture I would skip and dance in fun
O'er the slopes within the valley by the stream of Oregon.

When the sanguine flowering current paints each verdant copse with blood,
And the blushing salmon berry shows its stars within the wood,
And the yellow dandelion's shining in the mellow sun,
We are happy in our cottage by the stream of Oregon.

When the dogwood flowers are painted and hung
    among the trees,
With their broad and milky petals catching at the
    passing breeze,
And the snowy sweet syringa scents the very brooks
    that run,
It is ecstasy to wander by the stream of Oregon.

When the roses glow in Junetime all along the fences
    high,
And modest blue forgetmenots reflect the summer
    sky,
And mysterious mountain magnets are repressless
    wooing one,
I am glad my home is nestling by the stream of
    Oregon.

When the purple clover blossoms mingle with the
    meadow green,
And have spread a royal vesture over all the summer
    scene,
When the hay is sweetly curing in the glowing noon-
    day sun,
Then the air is full of fragrance by the stream of
    Oregon.

When the glorious vine maple paints each hill with
    brilliant hues,
And the harvest time is over and the bare feet seek
    their shoes,
And the snowy mountains glisten with the web the
    frost has spun,
There is plenty in the valley of the stream of Oregon.

So in comfort by the fireside of my cottage I will sit,
Looking o'er the fields and orchards of the flowing
    Willamette,

And I'll thank the Glorious Giver, when the course of life is run,
That my lines were laid in pleasure by the stream of Oregon.

THE UNLUCKY DAY.

I'm going to bed, I'm almost dead,
  I'm tired as I can be.
It's been the most unlucky day
  That ever I did see.
And everything from morn till night
  Has seemed to go just wrong,
Until I'm most discouraged
  Of trying to get along.

First Pa got up and built the fires,
  A half an hour about,
Then I got up and dressed me,
  The fires they both went out.
Then Pa came in and looked quite glum,
  I asked him what was wrong:
Some one had called at our hen house
  And took six hens along.

Then Ruthie tumbled down the stairs,
  And bumped her quite severe;
The boys were scuffling near the stove
  And broke my rocking chair;
The dog tramped down my choicest plants,
  The cow broke through the gate,
And tore up peas, and beans, and corn,
  At a disgusting rate.

The clothes line fell down in the dirt,
  The suds boiled on my feet;
We did not need one misery
  To make the day complete.

But Mooley thought 'twould do us good
  To bear a little more,
And so at night she kicked the milk
  All over on the floor.

And so I said I'll go to bed
  Or I shall surely weep,
But maybe I'll forget my grief
  If I can go to sleep.
Then I will gladly bid good night
  To this unlucky day,
With head and body aching sore
  I'll slowly creep away.

VICTORIA ARM.

Oh, I long to follow your windings away
To the depths of the forest some beautiful day;
To sit in my boat with my oars dipped deep,
And pull to the nooks where your dark waters sleep;
To watch (while the whistling whirlpools go by
In our pathway of bubbles reflecting the sky)
The mansions and cottages nestling among
Such scenes as the poets most often have sung;
Where the lawns sloping down to your waters are
  seen,
And are clothing your borders in carpets of green;
Where the rocks brown and mossy are washed by
  your stream,
And basking in sunlight the gulls ever dream.

I would bend to my oars and my boat it should go
With the foam on its bow like a drift in the snow,
To some spot in your shades where in langor I'd lie
With my hat o'er my eyes and look up at the sky,
And dream of some fairy land picture afar,
Where scenes ever tranquil and rapturous are;
Or swing at my painter in some sheltered nook
While I bury my mind in the leaves of a book;
Or go to the grounds where the picnickers meet
To waste summer hours with frolicking feet.
To your gorge I would go where waters rush through
And my boat cleaves the tide like a shaft from a bow,
And then floating in on the flood I would dream
  Where pastures and meadows come down to your
  stream;
Where the farmhouse and orchard entrancingly glide
On our view as we lazily drift with the tide.

Where waters rush through.

Where the forest-fringed lake lies sleeping before,
Its mirror all green from the trees on the shore.

Oh, a day on your bosom, my pride and my love
Is a day stolen down from the ether above,
And if I for your joys must the penalty pay,
Then a word of complaining I never shall say,
But guilty I'll plead to the thrall of your charm,
To the hours of delight on this beautiful Arm.

THE NOISY WORLD.

Did you ever think what a noisy place
  This old world is to-day?
And did you ever stop and think
  How still it used to be?

The great steamships now plow the sea
  With the roar of fire and steam.
Then, white-sailed boats o'er the ocean wave
  Glode like a silent dream.

Then, travelers o'er the earth passed slow
  In lumbering stage coach still,
Now, roaring trains with clang and screech
  Shake forest stream and hill.

Then, the weaver's loom and the blacksmith's forge
  And the lumber-maker's mill,
Made no more noise than the water wheel
  Or the twittering woodland rill,
But now great engines hiss and snort,
  And a million whistles scream
Until the earth seems all aroar
  Like a hideous nightmare dream.

Then, even war was a silent thing,
  With its clash of sword and spear,
And its loudest sound the bugle blast
  To fall on the listening ear.
Now cannon roars and rifle cracks,
  Like earthquakes shake the ground,
Until the earth with ague rolls
  And the sky seems falling down.

And still the earth's no happier
   Than in the silent days,
When men were content with simple joys
   And restful quiet ways.

And so the world goes roaring on,
   While the weary years roll round,
Until the voice of Gabriel's trump
   Shall silence every sound.
And the people wait with bated breath
   For the greatest crash of all,
When the Great, Great King shall take control
   And the kings of earth shall fall.

THE OLD SWIMMING HOLE.

Yes, Jim, my mind goes back to-day,
  To thirty years ago,
When you and I a swimming went
  So often, don't you know.
I'll ne'er forget the swimming hole,
  Down past the meadow green,
Where shimmering in the summer sun,
  The sand bars' backs were seen.

What times we had those glowing days,
  At the old swimming hole.
When, gently wooed by witching June,
  We out of school had stole.
And how we stretched out on the sand,
  Our backs all gleaming bare,
As, while the sun danced on our forms,
  We tried to dry our hair.

It would not do to travel home,
  With locks all streaming wet,
For sure those curls of moistened hair
  Would out our secret let.
But as we wound our homeward way,
  A strange sensation crept
Across our boyish shoulder blades,
  As tenderly we stepped.

At supper time, some one would touch
  Us gently on the back;
Our shirts seemed strangely heavy—
  We tried to make them slack.

It seemed as though some hideous spell
  Had crept in to our skins,
Which made us squirm and wriggle like
  A million burning pins.

At bedtime things had got so bad
  The burning made us scream,
And we were glad when mother came
  To spread our backs with cream.
The secret out, we spent the night
  In painful groaning thought,
And many days, with backs curved up,
  We sadly walked about.

Oh, how could I forget those days,
  We stole away from school,
When we would in the water plunge
  And on the sandbar roll,
When memory of the hours we spent
  Is printed on my soul,
By sunbeams through a smarting back
  Down at the swimming hole.

SHENANDOA.

Oh, Shenandoa, My Shenandoa!
When shall I ever see thee more?
When shall I wander as of old
Among thy meadows green and gold?
When shall I hear the whispering corn,
At dusky eve or dewy morn?
Or stand upon thy hills and view
Bewitching scenes forever new,
Below, where winds thy glimmering stream?

When shall I in the June time slip
Where pendant creepers in thee dip;
With book beneath the shade to lie,
And listen to thee gliding by?
Or in thy limpid depths to swim,
Below the arching willow's limb,
Where cattle in the noonday shade,
Contented, in thy waters wade?

When shall I hear the calling quail
Sit piping on the topmost rail?
Where sanguine sumach paints the hill,
Which echoed back the whistle shrill.
When shall I see thy crystal brooks,
Which twitter from among the oaks,
Or hear the rushing waters swish,
As round the rumbling wheels they push?

Oh, when shall I, with gladdened gaze,
Look up among thy mountains' haze,
Or on thy blooming farms below,
Between whose fields thy waters flow?

Oh, never will a sight more fair,
Though I may wander near and far,
Beguile the fleeting hours each day,
With raptures as they pass away.
Alack, my rural vale, I know
My aching feet can never go
A wandering, as they used to do,
Among thy mountains green and blue.
These eyes, I know, can never see
Your beauties, as they used to be;
But I can dream of scenes gone by,
Which raise the loving, longing sigh,
Though I should never see you more,
My Shenandoa, My Shenandoa,

TUMWATER.

Tumwater, with its tumbling stream,
A bower of spring, a summer dream;
Down deep among the hills of green,
The spray leaps up in rainbow sheen.
Then bending willows softly dip,
And kiss the river's blushing lip.
The summer sun with brow of red,
Beholds the sea and river wed.
There feathery cedar 'dorns the wood,
Above the cascade's murmuring flood.
The rock's rough cheek is damp with tears,
As he the river's sobbing hears.
And all delight the artist eye,
While fleecy summer clouds float by.
And fragrant breezes gently stir
The tresses of the stately fir.
All, All, breathe forth of quietude,
Which feeds the poet's pensive mood,
While dreaming of the virgin days
The forest and the stream have lost,
Amid the decades rushing past.

Tumwater with its tumbling stream.

JIM HEMSWORTH.

You may talk about your generals and admirals and such,
But according to my notion they don't amount to much.
I like the kind of courage that has learned to stand alone,
And doesn't need an army standing by to say well done.

Oh, certainly, this army grit is always well enough,
But still, in my opinion, it doesn't take the stuff
It does to face an awful death with no one by to see,
And cheer the heart with sympathy, whate'er the end may be.

Now there was brave Jim Hemsworth, at Young America,
Who jumped in to the jaws of death, only the other day;
He ran the crank above the shaft, the windlass, don't you know?
While Jimmy Smith and Frank Conson were working down below.

The crank snapped off when Jim hauled up a bucket full of rock
Just like a bullet from a gun; it was an awful shock.
The bucket shot toward the men with a terrific force,
Till Hemsworth jumped among the cogs and stopped its downward course.

They took him out his head dropped down upon his
    throbbing breast;
His arm was to his shoulder crushed, and torn his
    side and breast.
So tenderly they took him up and bore his form
    away,
And every eye was wet with tears on that terrific day.

And Smith and Conson couldn't talk whene'er they
    thought of him;
Their throats stopped with a rising lump; they owed
    their lives to Jim.
And so, you see, I came to think there's no one quite
    so brave
As is the man, who all alone, will jump a life to save.

While men with bugles blowing loud, and banners
    flying gay
May face the cannon's roaring mouth on some great
    battle day,
Still I admire the most the man who all alone can
    meet,
And lay, without a comrade's cheers, his life at duty's
    feet.

Fair Pend d'Orielle.

OLD TIGE.

You never heard tell of old yellow Tige,
  Of the Fifteenth army corps,
Who marched in the Red River campaign
  Of eighteen sixty-four?

Why, old Tige fed the boys on ham
  And mutton many a day,
That he stole from the officers' quarters
  In a most intelligent way.

The boys they thought as much of him
  As they could of any one,
And he knew his regiment as well
  As any other man.

He was wounded at Sabine Cross Roads,
  His leg was broken quite,
But the surgeon fixed it up with splints,
  And he was soon all right.

But every dog must meet his end,
  And Tige was like the rest,
And at Yellow Bayou, May eighteen
  He couldn't stand the test.

For his body wasn't bullet proof,
  And they filled him full of lead,
And many a cheek was wet with tears
  When the boys heard he was dead.

They gave him a soldier's funeral,
  When they laid him in the ground;

They fired a volley over his grave,
   While the mourners stood around.

And that's the story of old dog Tige,
   Who fought with the Fifteenth corps,
In the famous Red River campaign
   Of eighteen sixty-four.

THE PATIENT ONE.

Who is it, when the times are hard, and we can
    scarcely live,
Will never ask for anything, but always tries to give?
Who wears her last year's bonnet and goes without a
    cloak?
Who laughs about her worn-out gloves as though it
    were a joke?
        Why, Mother.

Who is it always says that Pa must be provided for,
And always have a coat and hat if nothing's left for
    her?
Who wants the children to look nice, no matter what
    she wears,
And always smiles and says "all right," and never
    shows she cares?
        Why, Mother.

Who is it drinks cold water when others must have
    milk,
And when there's only bread to eat will never cry or
    sulk?
Who waits upon the others, and never seems to tire,
And in the night when they are sick gets up and builds
    the fire?
        Why, Mother.

Who is it always stays at home when all the others go,
Who, if she wants to get outside no one will ever
    know?
Who darns and patches, mops and scrubs and combs
    the children's hair,

And sews on carpet-rags and knits when she has time
   to spare?
      Why, Mother.

Who keeps the supper warm for Pa whenever he's out
   late,
And when we have a treat she puts the nicest on his
   plate?
Who feeds the others often when she must go without,
So careful that her own regrets no one shall know
   about?
      Why, Mother.

Who'll have the freshest, greenest home in God's
   green Paradise?
Who'll have the finest mansion when she goes above
   the skies?
Who, if I have my way, wont have a single hand to
   stir,
And the youngest, fairest angels just to stand and wait
   on her?
      Why, Mother.

Sunset at Sitka.

THE TREMBLING WORLD.

A curious old world this is with all its funny works,
I wonder we're not all sea sick with all its jumps and jerks.
They say a stone thrown in the sea a thousand miles or more,
Will make a wave which circling will reach unto the shore.

And so they say a little jar upon the earth, though light,
Will circle clear around the globe from morning until night.
Now with so many thumps and knocks the earth must be shuck up
The whole endurin' blessed time, like water in a cup.

When some big man stomps down his foot to emphasize his talk—
There must be thousands doin' it while politicians walk.
And then just think of all the carts, and horses, too, there are,
They must shake up a lot of ground and give it quite a jar.

And then the cars a puffing and running o'er the ground—
The'd give the earth an ague shake with their great roaring sound;
And when the big guns boom again down at the trial yard,
It must shake up the bowels of the earth most awful hard.

And so I think it's strange, I say, that we're not sea
    sick quite,
With all this roar and clatter from morning until
    night;
For there's a constant banging on the surface of the
    earth,
To say nothing of the earthquakes from his inwards
    belching forth.
And if its true, that every jar is felt the world around,
We must be kept a shiv'ring from our heads down to
    the ground.

WHEN THE CROWS FLY HOME.

When the crows fly home the sun is low,
  Bringing western shadows near,
And the farmer listens in the field,
  The supper horn to hear.
    It is time for all to cease their toil,
    When the crows fly home.

When the crows fly home to the Carraboos,
  With many a caw and flap,
The busy mills will stop their hum,
  And the blacksmith cease his tap.
    Soon all the world will be at rest,
    When the crows fly home.

When the crows fly home the tide is in,
  The waves wash on the shore,
And to-day the birds on the bare tide flats
  Will search for food no more.
    The world will stop its strife for bread,
    When the crows fly home.

When the crows fly home, and I watch here
  Their rear guard out of sight,
Stealing up o'er the western hills,
  Come the vanguard shades of night.
    We welcome the restful twilight hour.
    When the crows fly home.

When the noisy crows have all flown home,
  The glittering stars shine bright,
And everything is silent,
  With the somber hush of night,
    The whole world sleeps in silence,
    When the crows have all flown home.

MARCH.

When Father Time called his daughter March,
  To come from her winter bed,
She shyly peeped at the drifting snow,
  Then covered up her head.

But he called again, more urgently,
  For the cold from the northeast swept,
And she groaned as from the frosty quilts
  The shivering maiden crept.

For a time she shivered around the fire
  But borrowed winter's cloak,
And faced the frowns of the world outside
  Then her sister spring awoke.

The days grew warm, and the sun came out,
  And gentle Chinook came too.
The earth and sky grew soft and warm,
  And mellow breezes blew.

The moon and frost made a heartless plan,
  And chilled the glowing nights,
But each passing day was a golden dream,
  With budding spring's delights.

The sky looked at the sea and blushed,
  As the sun crept into bed,
The sea looked back and her face became
  A rosy, rosy red.

The winter cloak has now been packed
  Away with camphor balls,
While roguish March has softly purloined
  The April shower which falls.

And so the whole world wandering out,
  Mid flowers to dream and delve,
Vote daughter March of '96,
  The fairest of the twelve.

Blaine, Wash.

And you, St. Helens, must you stand
In front of Adams, airs so grand,
Because you are a little taller;
I'm sure his lessons are no smaller.

Then "Mr. Olympus?" Schucksan asks,
"Can I be counted in the class?"
"Silence, sir!" the teacher roared,
"Such impudence I can't afford.
"If I am short you'll find I'm able
"To run correct the teacher's table."

The little fellows up in line
Then tried to wear demeanors fine;
The teacher standing out in front,
They feared with all his manners blunt;
And silence fell on all the school,
While the grim master took his stool.

MY TWINING ROSE.

There sprung by our lowly cottage door
A plant as fair as e'er seen before.
We tenderly nursed it day by day,
And the joyful years thus passed away,
As sweet it garnished the fleeting hours,
We longed to see it adorned with flowers.

It bloomed one day with blossoms fair
As flowers that grow where angels are.
Oh, how we joyed in that sweet rose tree,
Which bloomed alone for us to see;
And spoke our delight, yes, o'er and o'er,
As it twinned and blossomed about our door.

We lived so much in our lovely prize,
That we knew not the gaze of envious eyes.
As it bloomed most fair on a sad bright day,
One softly came and bore it away;
And left the door of my cottage bare,
And we to weep for our rose so rare.

I wandered out, with my heart all dew,
To try and find where my sweet flower grew;
Till at last I came to a city grand,
Where a river rippled o'er golden sand;
And there I found, where a throng could see,
By a palace, bloomed my white rose tree.

I said, as I saw the delighted throng.
Stop and admire as they passed along:
"Ah, me, ah, me, it is better so,

"Than that I should enjoy you alone below;
"So blush and bloom, and perfume the air
"For the heavenly throng in the City fair."

ACER CIRCINATUM.

A grand bouquet on every hill
   The bright vine-maple stands;
With blended colors exquisite
   From nature's painter's hands.

The glory of the autumn now
   With royal tints aglow,
Acer circinatum shines
   Wherever we may go.

With royal purple, orange, too,
   Her robe is woven well.
And scarlet, yellow, green and gold,
   With skill we cannot tell.

So I'll not try to picture all
   The glories she can show,
Through all the months of autumn,
   E'er robbed by blustering snow.

FLORA MACDONALD.

Flora Macdonald is lovely,
  Flora Macdonald is fair
And she has twinkles in her feet
  And sunshine in her hair.
Her eyes are as blue as a patch of sky
  Through a fluffy summer cloud,
And they sparkle and dance
  As I look at her, with my heart to her beauty bowed.

Her cheek is like a blushing rose,
  But the colors come and go,
As the waves in grass in summer time,
  When the gentle breezes blow.
Her lips would tempt a heart more cold
  Than mine to stoop and taste,
But she did not know how she tempted me,
  As I looked in her lovely face.

You would like to know where my Flora lives,
  And see her bewitching charms
And make the roses come in her cheek
  As her smile your bosom warms?
She dwells in the Queen City fair,
  By the side of the deep blue sea,
And I met her on a quaint back street,
  The day that she captured me.

Oh, no, there is no danger there,
  For she's only four years old,
And never heard of the Wizard Seer
  Who sang to the Scots so bold—
Of the other Flora Macdonald,

Who couldn't have been more fair,
Though she fought for Culloden's pretender
  With a courage grand and rare.

But my Flora Macdonald is lovely,
  My Flora Macdonald is fair,
And I'll never forget her blue, blue eye,
  Or the sunshine in her hair.
That vision of baby lovliness,
  I met on Beacon Hill.
Oft' on a dreamy summer day
  I think I can see her still.
And though she grow to a woman grand,
  Or perchance to one more plain,
I never expect with delight to gaze
  On a child more fair again.

    Victoria, June, 1885.

FISHING.

Did you ever go a-fishing with a slender bamboo pole,
And when you didn't get a bite just throw it in the hole?
Did you ever fish and fish and fish and never get a bite;
Then hang around the creek all day and come home in the night?

Did you ever go a-fishing and leave your pole behind,
And with your knife a sapling cut, the best that you could find,
And hold it up above the stream till you were tired out,
And then go whistling home again without a single trout?

Did you ever fish four days in five—you stole the time to go,
And never catch a mess of fish that you would care to show?
And then the fifth come proudly home, while flapping at your side,
Would hang a string of beauties that you didn't care to hide?

Your reputation then was made, and no one knew the days
That you had tired, hungry, mad, come home by secret ways;
Nor what these fish had cost you, of time, chagrin and such;
Your reputation wasn't made by fish you didn't catch.

JEALOUSY.

Thou art a crawling, creeping worm,
A specter for the soul's alarm;
A carrion bird to seek for stenchful food;
A goblin of fear to spoil the greenest wood;
A nothing but a great geboo,
To worry grown up children as you do;
Your food is black suspicion foul,
Your sweetest song but a discordant howl.
You daub the purest acts with slime;
Your spleen is vent without regard to time.
Your dearest work is in your garden, hate,
Where you're employed both early and both late,
To raise a bitter vegetable called—well,
There is no need its name the world to tell.

You make a man a stubborn beast, a mule,
A coward, sneaking mangy cur and fool;
A boor, a slanderer, with lost self-respect,
Who murders her whom he's sworn to protect.
A runaway, with carriage smashed, and reins,
And tearing down the street to dash out his own brains.
With all behind of peace and love and truth,
And all before of fear and hate and death.

Of woman you have made a snarling cat,
Who sends suspicious glances other women at,
A tigress, filled with fear and spite and sin,
She paces up and down her den within;
Rob her of reason and respect of age,
Feed her suspicion and foul hate and rage.
Faith, love and trust behind, forgotten name
All, all before her fear and death and shame.

OAK AND IVY.

In the forest grew an oak tree all alone;
Of a thousand other oak trees he was one,
    But his heart was fancy free;
    He a bachelor would be
Till he found a mate attractive for his own.

The other trees this sturdy oak did flout,
And said a mate to get he should about;
    But he waved his arms in glee,
    And he said "I would be free,
Till my heart feels its affection going out."

An ivy grew beside the oak tree's feet,
And it smelled the flowers and clover growing sweet,
    But it loved the sturdy oak,
    As it cast its upward look;
In his arms it dreamed of happiness complete.

So the ivy clung around his noble form,
Unrepulsed and never thought of any harm,
    For the oak tree loved to have
    Her seek his protection brave,
While they felt the summer breezes soft and warm.

So the ivy always clung about her love,
Till their lives appeared for ever interwove;
    They mumured soft and sweet,
    That their love was quite complete,
While the forest whispered softly, "we approve."

But while the ivy clung upon her love,
There was, gnawing at his vitals from above,

A disease that should bring low
His proud form upon the snow,
When the winter blasts across the plain should move.

Still the loving ivy clung upon his form,
As if to shield him from all threatening harm,
But he could not cling to her,
Though he felt affection stir,
And knew he could not breast the winter's storm.

Thus when the cold December breezes blew,
Sad, sad at heart the clinging ivy knew
That she could not save her love,
No matter how she strove
To comfort him with her affection true.

Prostrate he lay upon the frozen earth,
Until the spring to budding flowers gave birth;
But still clinging to his form,
As though his love to warm,
The ivy reached her springing tendrils forth.

But at last she knew that death had claimed her love;
Her affection began to gaze and rove;
A chestnut growing near,
Seemed unto her very dear,
So she ran and sought his sheltering arms above.

BOUTONIERE.

My three little girls they ran to-day
To bring me a buttonhole bouquet;
They gathered the blossoms in bunches three,
With love in their dear little hearts for me.

They brought their offerings one by one,
With faces aglow in the springtime sun,
And eyes as bright as the flowers they bring,
And voices as sweet as the birds can sing.

My darling Ruth, the youngest of them,
Held a pansy up with a very short stem.
I couldn't grieve her loving heart;
It must make of my boutoniere a part.

Jane brought a primrose like herself,
And a wallflower sweet, the dear little elf.
Of course for them I must find a place,
To keep the smile on her loving face.

Then with a rosebud and sweet pea
My Marguerite came with delight to me,
And laid in my hand her offerings fair,
While she brushed away her curling hair.

I could not reject a single flower
To spoil for one that happy hour,
So I said, while my buttonhole was full,
"My dear little girls, I will take them all."

Oconta Gorge, Columbia River.

*THE HARP OF THE SANDS.

I sat one night where the flowing tide
  Came in at the Golden Gate,
And listened to the restless sea,
  Though the hour was growing late.

The earth was still, the ocean calm,
  The air was soft and low,
And the only thing that made a sound
  Was the creeping water's flow.

A ship passed in the dusk along,
  Like a phantom up the bay,
Its tall masts mirrored in the deep,
  While it slipped in the gloom away.

The sea birds chattered, as they flew,
  In whispering notes of night,
Or sat on the bosom of the deep,
  When the moon came into sight.

The porpoise flashing in and out,
  Far off on the distant sea,
With all the other ocean sights,
  Made an evening show for me.

And so I sat and listened to
  The ocean's mighty swells,
The story which the sea's unrest,
  Forever throbbing, tells.

---

*Facts.

And then I walked in the soft moonlight,
   And listened to the tide,
As it glided in through the Golden Gate,
   From the ocean green and wide.

At last I stopped and held my breath,
   For a strain of music came,
Like the wind through strings Aeolian,
   Too sweet to have a name.

And sad and low it floated up,
   From the ocean-dampened sands,
Like a harp thrust out from the hurrying deep
   And played by unseen hands.

I stood and listened to the strains,
   I had one time heard before,
To the harp of the sands played by unseen hands,
   In the rocks along the shore.

The hour was right, for alone at night
   Will the sand harps ever play;
When the flowing tide begins to glide
   Into the shadowy bay.

I listened wrapt to the sad, sweet strain,
   For I knew when the tide was in
No more would the sand harp play for me,
   By the fingers soft unseen.

Nor could I hear in the daylight glare
   This music of the night,
For the glowing sun would, soaring high,
   Give the wierd musicians fright.

So I drank my fill till the music ceased,
  And I knew I should hear no more,
Then back to the city I took my way,
  Along the rock-bound shore.

COLORED NOISE.

'Twas in a farmhouse chamber room some thirty years ago,
The earth was frozen up outside and covered white with snow.
Four boys had been tucked snugly in for ten long winter hours,
But now the prying glance of dawn had roused them from their snores.

They stood about the stovepipe warm on one foot or on two,
As slow slid on a trouser leg or foot slipped in a shoe.
But suddenly there came a whack, a pillow fair and square,
Aimed with a careful boyish hand, struck Tom across the ear.

Of course the pillow must go back, and thus the fight began,
And thick the feathery bundles flew like popcorn in a pan.
Sometimes the boys were on the floor and sometimes on the bed,
And while the battle fiercely raged the noise grew very red.
At last a gentle, soft, gray noise came floating from below,
And mother kindly plead with them, "oh, boys, please don't do so."
A lull fell on the mad career for full a minute then,
But blood was up, and soon anew the battle raged again.

Oh, come where the palm trees fringe the shore of the mighty Golden State.

The fight bid fair to work distress with mother's pillows there,
When suddenly a great black noise came rolling up the stair.
As through the open chamber door came father's angry head,
Four half dressed boys, with puff and pant, rolled nimbly into bed.

Like prairie dogs they disappeared within their tumbled nest,
And—well, I wish with all my heart, I needn't tell the rest,
For father's hand was large and hard, the boys not over dressed;
Humiliation met us there, if it must be confessed.

And then there fell above the stairs a silence cold and white
When father, with a warning brown, had vanished out of sight.
And meditation was the rule around the stovepipe then,
While sad and slow the boys commenced to dress themselves again.

THE CALIFORNIA LETTER.

Everywhere else in this country a California letter is known by a peculiar perfume which it exhales; a perfume which seems a combination of the scents of orange, banana, pomegranate and apple, and is as mysterious as a dream, as it floats out when the letter is opened.

He came to her bedside so gently,
  Laid a hand on her feverish brow,
And said, while he touched her soft bandaged eyes,
  I've something here, sweet, for you now.

"I've a letter, my wife, with sweet odors rife,
  "And the scent its envelope exhales
"Might come on a breeze from the isles of the blessed,
  "And reminds me of strange fairy tales.

"There are roses and lilies and sweet apple flowers
  "Hid away mid its secret perfumes,
"Pomegranates and palms float my visions before,
  "Or the groves where the orange tree blooms.

"Can you guess the fair clime where this letter so
      "sweet
  "Folds away mid its odorous reams
"Perfumes from Araby or Italy's shores,
  "Which waken the heart's warmest dreams?"

"Place it here," said the wife, "though I cannot behold
  "I may its sweet odors inhale,
"By aroma of fruits and attar of flowers,
  "Let it tell me its exquisite tale.

"Oh, I see, as I catch the perfume laden breath,
  "California's rivers of gold;
"Her mountains, her valleys, her fruits and her flowers
  "Entranced does my vision behold.

"No land so bewitches by sending its breath
  "Imprisoned in letters so far.
"I know without guessing my letter's from where
  "California's orange groves are."

MOTHER DOESN'T WANT ME.

In a swimmin'? I don't know
Whether I had best to go,
Here's a dand'lion let me blow
　And see if mother wants me.

Wait a little, let me be,
In a minute I will see,
If I can blow it off at three,
　Then I am sure she wants me.

One, good rousing puff, oh my,
See the downy seed wings fly,
Can't do better if I try,
　Then I'm afraid she wants me.

Two, and nearly all are gone;
One more blow and then I'm done;
If I do it then I'll run
　Home, cause mother wants me.

Three, and that's the very last,
Still some seeds are sticking fast;
Guess I'll go 'f I didn't ast,
　Cause mother doesn't want me.

FARMER BLUE.

A very good neighbor was our Farmer Blue,
And a very fine man, as everyone knew;
But, would you believe it? every one said
That our Farmer Blue was always afraid.
Not of bad, savage beasts, and never had been,
Nor of ugly, or fighting or blustering men.
The forest most dark had no terrors for him,
And 'twas he that talked reason to Bitter Creek Jim.

But every one said, and it was quite a shock,
(Specially to his wife) he was 'fraid of his stock.

You see, Billy Blue was a cobbler by trade,
And had left the old farm when a lusty young lad.
But a tramp came along one cold winter day,
And he hadn't the heart to turn him away,
So he took him in kindly and gave him the best,
A strong pair of shoes and a good coat and vest.

Mr. Blue in his kindness thought nothing of that,
But the tramp, it seems certain, he never forgot,
For one day, ten years after, or possibly more,
A lawyer man called at the shoemaker's door.

"I've a will," said the lawyer, "at my office down town,
"In which you are mentioned, so please call around."
The will duly read, showed Billy the heir
To a beautiful farm worth ten thousand or more.
"All stocked up, with buildings and everything fine,"
Said the lawyer, "and better than any gold mine."

The tramp had gone west, and in Iowa soil
Had delved out a fortune by vigilent toil,

But the seeds of disease had weakened his frame,
And dying he thought of good Billy Blue's name.
So his will, when 'twas read, showed that everything went
To our friend, William Blue, of Pawlet, Vermont.

The question which rose in the minds of the Blues,
When sure of the truth of the wonderful news,
Was, what should be done with the acres out west?
Should they sell them, or work them, or what would be best?

Billy's wife was for farming, with emphasis, too,
But Billy would sell them, he very well knew,
And build them a house and keep on at his trade,
For to "tackle" new business he felt quite afraid.

But his wife won the day when it came to the test,
So they packed up their goods and migrated out west;
And this is the story, not long, but quite true,
How Billy became Farmer William J. Blue.

And, sad to relate, Mr. Blue was afraid
Of the stock on the farm, which he so wished to trade.
Afraid that the cows would hook or would kick,
And his horror of hogs made the farmer quite sick.

The horses were terrors he hated to touch;
They knew it, and kept him a thinking them such.
The sheep he was certain would bunt him in two,
And near them he never knew what he should do.

And even the geese he watched with respect;
Never neared an old hen, but he feared he'd be pecked.

So you see that the farm was no paradise fair,
To Billy, whose life was a constant nightmare.

To please his dear wife he most certainly tried,
But try all he would, his fear would not hide,
Though she laughed at his fears and had none herself,
Still, his joy was all gone, laid away on a shelf.

For five years she tried to make out of him
A farmer, but failed to get him in trim,
So at last she gave up in alarm and dispair,
Determined whatever he choose she would share.

The farm it was sold, with its terrible stock;
With the money a pretty town cottage they bought;
And a shop, where our Billy could peg at his shoes,
With nothing to frighten or give him the blues.

So now, when you're passing along on the street,
You will hear a man's whistle quite happy complete.
He pegs, sings and whistles the merry hours through,
For Billy no longer is scared Farmer Blue.

THE GIRL WHO SWEEPS MY ROOM.

How still she goes about the house
    With dusting pan and pail and broom;
She steps as light as any mouse,
    The girl who sweeps and dusts my room.

How nice she is with couch and chair,
    How careful fixes everything
Just as it was, with conscience rare,
    Why should I not her praises sing?

That book upon the writing stand,
    The lamp and matches, pen and ink,
Are placed again by her deft hand
    So of the change I'd never think.

These pictures on the bureau here,
    Just as I leave them I will find;
My pen and paper, never fear,
    Will never feel her touches kind,
Or if they do no one would know
    (Except the dust was brushed away,
And all her task completed so)
    That she'd been in the room to-day.

As graceful as her mountain birch,
    Is she who tidies up my room;
Her quiet face (I see it such)
    As Norseland flowers in Dovre bloom.

Her brow, as open highland fjeld,
    And nothing hidden there can be;
No truer bosom ever swelled

Than her's who sweeps my room for me.
Her eyes as blue as her own fjords,
  Which nestle deep mid Norway's hills,
I cannot picture by mere words,
  My pen, at best but poorly tells.

And so she goes about the house,
  With dusting pan and pail and broom,
And cheerful all her duty does—
  The girl who dusts and sweeps my room.

TWO SPIRITS WITHIN.

"Two spirits struggle within you?" What, only two?
  Well, if 'twere only a pair to conquer, 'twould be
    quite easy to do.
But when it's two hundred spirits dancing to and fro,
You find yourself, of all the earth, the hardest person
    to know.
"Two spirits struggle within you;" how fortunate,
    indeed.
You must find yourself, on the whole of earth's shelf,
    the easiest book to read,
For them you have two hands to match, two feet to
    flee away,
Two ears to hear, two eyes to watch, so let them
    enjoy their play.

But, alas for me! with my two hundred struggling
    within;
What can I do to overcome their terrible silent din?
A harp of a thousand strings am I; like a dry leaf
    tossed about,
Now tell me, how will ever I my secret self find out?

Mt. Baker, seen from Gulf of Georgia.

HAPPY IN BLAINE.

Oh, a happy folk are we in Blaine,
Mid summer sun and winter rain;
We laugh and sing as the days go by,
And our bosoms never heave a sigh.

Would you know what makes us free from care,
And every day in the whole year fair,
And our hearts as light as they can be,
And our forms so plump and round to see?

It is because the hateful form
Of hunger never threatens harm,
And the raving wolf, he never comes
To stand before our happy homes.

Our store is always running o'er,
And the tide goes out and opens the door;
Then all to do is to help ourselves
From off the free and low-hung shelves.

There tender bivalves rich and rare
Send fountains spraying high in air,
And the huntsman armed with spade and pail
Knows well his quest will never fail.

The sideling crab shies swift away,
In the sea weed meadow at his play.
The flounder skims along the sands,
And comes to the reach of eager hands.
The sardine swarms and the salmon leaps
Above the halibut's pasture deeps.
The fisher combs the willing sea,

And knows while he shakes his comb that he
Will have by night his boat well full,
And home with the tide he'll gaily pull.

The mighty sturgeon churns the sea,
But fried in his own rich fat will be.
The tom cod glides among the piles,
Nor heeds the fisher's sleepy wiles,
And comes ashore with the greatest ease,
In companies of twos and threes.
And the toothsome smelt with rash delight,
Leaps out upon the dry sands quite,
And goes to the seeker's pail aloft,
Who walks in the autumn sunlight soft.

And so I say to you again,
That we are happy folks in Blaine,
Nor heed the toils and strifes outside,
While we watch the flow of our teeming tide.

NO HOME.

"A home, a home," the heart of man
  Craves only "give to me a home."
To seek it he will wander far,
  And over all creation roam.

Since God in wrath at Babel's tower
  Taught him the folly of his way,
His face has ever more been turned
  Toward the glowing close of day.

Man looks upon the rising sun,
  And greets the morn with fresh delight,
But hopes to lay his burdens down,
  And taste the comforts of the night.

And so his gaze he's ever cast
  In search of comforts peace and rest,
Where bright hope's finger pointed him,
  Toward the sunset-painted west.

He trod the mountains and the plains
  Until he reached the restless sea,
Then wondered, with a strange unrest,
  What secret there beyond could be.

And so he crossed the sighing deep,
  And sought the mists of other shores,
Among the new world's mysteries
  To search the depth of hidden stores.

Forward the sunset's magnet draws
  Across the rivers, hills and vales,

And yet, in longing for a home
  He still attempts but always fails.

At last he sees the hope is vain,
  "There is no home, alas," he cries,
(The toil is all without reward)
  "Beneath the everlasting skies."

Mt. Hood from Portland.

THE RIDE OF FORTY-TWO.

The whole world's heard of the wonderful ride of bold Phil Sheridan,
And Paul Revere and his midnight flight makes the pulses leap again;
And how the wild six hundred rode into the jaws of death—
When told by one who saw the deed, makes the listener hold his breath.

Those deeds were grand and those heroes great who rode their steeds to fame,
But I will write on the page to-day another hero's name;
How he climbed the snowy mountain peaks and faced the blizzard's roar,
To save for the glorious flag he loved the ever vernal shore.

Did you ever hear of the mighty ride that Marcus Whitman made?
How he faced death's elements alone and of nothing seemed afraid?
How he sprang into the saddle on that frosty autumn day,
To ride to the nation's capital, four thousand miles away?

Have you ever heard how he galloped off from the shores of evergreen,
To the lands where no sheltering mountain peaks the howling blizzards screen;

Where icy streams across his way swept dark and threatening,
While his good steed bore him forward on his journey hastening?

And have you heard of the faithful hearts who followed his return
Across the barren sand, where the Western deserts burn;
Through rugged mountain passes to the stream of Oregon,
Where the turbulent Pacific wave embraces the setting sun?

Well, so it was, and thus I sing how Marcus Whitman pressed,
Where death lurked in the mountain peaks and icy river's breast;
How he willingly the dangers faced, as he turned from his own fireside,
Into the blasts of winter away from his loving bride.

So while the tales of daring deeds our throbbing pulses swell,
We'll think of the ride from sea to sea that Whitman made so well;
And how he saved to the starry flag the land of the Chinook,
With a bravery that none can tell in song or story book.

STRAY SHEEP.

Man is a harp of a thousand strings.
Woman is a harp of ten thousand strings.

* * *

If a man trusts God he is what God makes him.
If a man does not trust God he is what he makes himself.

* * *

God's poor are blessed.
The world's poor are cursed.

* * *

My dear, there is a great deal of one's soul in the touch of one's hands.

* * *

How much like angels devils act sometimes.

* * *

The life of a man commences at marriage; the first ten years he is wedded to his wife, the next twenty to his children and to his business, the fourth decade to retrospect and the fifth to life.

* * *

My Epitaph—He wrote a line which gave birth to a thought.

* * *

'Tis better to have lived to fall—
To rise again—than never to have lived at all.

* * *

Oft' when the heart is most full the pen is most empty.

* * *

He is truly great who can stand the test of prosperity.

* * *

A few years of poverty should be the school in

which we are fitted for either earthly or eternal prosperity.

* * *

Never let your own physical condition govern your behavior toward others.

* * *

God has so arranged it that he who leaves "footprints on the sands of time" is more certain to leave footprints on the golden sands of eternity.

* * *

A crafty person is seldom a shrewd one.

* * *

Dotards boast of what they have done; fools of what they intend to do.

* * *

'Tis well to leave some "footprints on the sands of time" to prove
That our lives have made us worthy to walk the fields above.

* * *

Never tell anything but the truth, but do not always tell the truth.

* * *

Where justice rules there would I abide.

* * *

Never play with fire or water. If your companions play with fire provide yourself with a blanket; if they play with water get out of the boat and upon the land as soon as possible.

* * *

Forget about yourself as much as possible.

* * *

He was a good fellow, but he never moved so fast as he did on the day of his funeral.

* * *

Oh, for the day when doubt shall be removed.
And sin shall be abhorred and virtue loved;

When God in power shall be a guide indeed,
And each his loving words shall ever heed.

* * *

Love in me is justice to my child. Love in my child is obedience to me.

Love in God is justice. Love in God's children is obedience.—I. John v., 2-3.

* * *

Deceit, thy name is woman.
Conceit, thy name is man.

* * *

Hope looks forward.
Despair looks backward.

* * *

Stand alone. If you lean against something you are likely to defile yourself, for even whitewash sumetimes rubs off. But if you must lean on something, lean upon God; He will support without contaminating.

SNOQUALMIE.

Oh, come, my friend and follow me
Where plays the stream Snoqualmie,
  Where o'er the cliffs the waters flow,
  Mad leaping to the rocks below,
  And snowy mists the breezes blow,
    Where now my dreams are calling me.

Come then, my friend and follow me
Where plays the stream Snoqualmie,
  So great its noise that all is still
  In vale and forest, rock and hill,
  And whirling waters drown my will,
    Where now my dreams are calling me.

Come, come, my friend, and follow me
Where plays the stream Snoqualmie,
  Its raging waters madly tossed,
  And other sounds all dead and lost,
  And lips give but a sound at most,
    Where now my dreams are calling me.

Then come, my friend and follow me
Where plays the stream Snoqualmie,
  With me to-day and pass an hour,
  Lost where a world of waters roar
  As plunging from the rocks they pour,
    Where now my dreams are calling me.

Oh, come then, come and follow me
Where plays the stream Snoqualmie,
  Upon the bough the screeching jay
  Is like to drive my dreams away,
  Unless you come with me to-day
    Where now my dreams are calling me.

Oh, come, my friend, and follow me
Where plays the stream Snoqualmie.

WHAT PUFFS UP?

Did you ever see a bullet larger than the gun that fired it?
Did you ever see an egg larger than the bird that laid it?
Did you ever see a creature bigger than the God who made it?
Did you ever see a baby that was larger than its mother?
Did you ever see a ship that was larger than the ocean?
Did you ever see a mountain that was larger than the earth?
Or a thought that was larger than the mind that gave it birth?
Did you ever see a loaf that was larger than the flour?
Yes? 'Twas larger, true it is, but 'twas gas that made it more.
So a man is swelled with nothing when his heart is puffed with pride;
When he lets the smoke from hades his Redeemer's glories hide.
And he'd better train with vigor or his superfluous weight
Down deep into perdition will drag him to his fate.

FRIENDS.

(Dedicated to C. W. C. and G. W. C.)

Our friends are those who share with us
  The bitter and the sweet,
Who warmly take us by the hand
  When we reverses meet.
They are the ones whose hearts are warm
  Through all adversity;
For we suffered all together
  In the crash of ninety-three.

Prosperity was smiling bright,
  We all enjoyed her cheer,
And thought our friends were plentiful,
  And we had naught to fear;
We little dreamed in those old days
  What trials there should be—
That many would not stand the test
  In the crash of ninety-three.

But so it was, and those we thought
  Would cling through thick and thin,
Were first to turn their backs on us
  When trouble had begun.
They had a look of sadness then
  Most pitiful to see,
And blamed their neighbors for their woes,
  In the crash of ninety- three.

But, praise the Lord, we had our friends
  Who took things as they came,
And when the storm was howling round
  Proved worthy of the name;

Who said, while warmly clasping hands,
  In the old friendly way:
"We suffered all together
  In the crash of ninety-three."

RIBES SANGUINEUM.

While other flowers are still asleep,
  While frost is on the rills,
Sprinkled among the evergreens,
  Glory of the hills.
Blushes of the youngest spring,
  Your buds are bursting green
And promising to clothe the earth
  The fairest ever seen.

No fairer flowers adorn the wood,
  In any favored spot,
Than our own bright sanguineum,
  With blushing blooms, I wot.
It brightens up each shadowy nook;
  It clothes the sunny hills
With varigated blushing pink,
  Each heart with pleasure fills.

First offering of gentle spring,
  Bestowed with lavish hand,
Makes brave the other flowers to come,
  And helps to cheer the land.
Your bright racemes of blushing stars
  Have all a beauty rare.
Vivid and soft and delicate,
  And perfect as you are.

And so we sing a song to you,
  Our bright sanguineum,
For when we see your blushes rare
  We know that spring has come.

SELLING THE WEE ONE'S PETS.

There, they've taken them off—
All my beautiful hens;
  There's Brindle, and Top-Knot and Gray.
And their nice little feet
All tied with old strings
  Just to keep them from flying away.

And now they can't scratch
Any more in the yard—
  Oh, dear, mama, what will we do?
And Brindle won't come
Through the back kitchen door
  And scamper about when I shoo.

She had tears in her eyes—
They tumbled her so—
  Be careful! They just didn't try.
And now I am so mad
'Cause they acted so bad,
  That, mama, I b'lieve I could cry.

Do you think I want Twiggs?
No, he's only a cat.
  I want back my chickens theirself;
And I don't like the cat,
Oh, take him away—
  He'll be sure to climb up on the shelf.

And you think they'll be good
To my Top-Knot and Speck?
  Well, I don't; they acted so rough.
And they made Brindle squall

When they pulled her about—
And don't you think that was enough?

Yes, and I want them all.
No, just one ain't enough,
  For she would be lonesome and sad.
Bring back every one,
(But now I'll be still).
  If you do I'll be awfully glad.

There she lies on the floor,
Mamma's prop'd up her head.
  All forgotten her chickens so dear,
In the midst of her grief
She has fallen asleep—
  On her cheek there's but one little tear.

Reveille Island, Lake Whatcom.

The lilly, in the summer sun,
　Looks upward with its yellow eyes.

The blue kingfisher perching low
　Heeds watchfully the minnows play,
Then darting to the limpid depths
　With screech of triumph is away.

The mountains, sky and silent moon
　Are pictured softly in my lake;
All silent float across my view
　As I their beauties there partake.

A ruthless breeze breaks on the scene,
　And with its rude encircling arms
Forecasts the day when human hands
　Will rob my lake of half its charms.

MY BICYCLE.

It seems to me no bird could be
  More light than I to-day,
While mounted on my flying wheel
  I swiftly skim away.

Some pinioned soul has winged itself
  Into my bounding heart,
For flying to my farthest veins
  My blood does leap and start.

I feel, as tree and glade and glen
  Go gliding swiftly by,
With but a pair of feathered wings
  I'd soar up to the sky.

I lend my power unto my wheel
  It pays me in delight,
And thus together swift we go
  From morning until night.

I'm free, free, free from all the cares
  Of plodding human flesh,
As I upon my bicycle
  Sweep forward as I wish.

To sail in boat across the wave
  Seems imbecilic sport,
And of the silent, sweeping wheel
  It comes supremely short.

To carriage ride is lazy joy
  With independence gone,

And by a sweating panting steed
   Its comfort must be won.

The orasman is a plodder slow
   Upon the rushing stream,
A plunge into the aqueous flood
   May dampen all his dream.

A weary, crawling, crushed snail
   Is the pedestrian,
Who slowly measures off the space
   In the old fashioned plan.

The steamboat and the railway cars
   Are but a weary mode
To locomote about the world,
   Their joys are but a load.

Oh give to me my willing wheel,
   Its soft pneumatic tires,
Kindle within my bounding heart
   Heaven's ethereal fires.

It has within its quivering frame
   And swiftly turning wheel
The essence of all earthly joys,
   That mortal man can feel.

"What is trouble?"

TROUBLE.

"What is trouble?" she asked me,
   My four-year-old daughter Ruth,
As she sat by the fire in a study brown—
   This youthful seeker for truth.

I thought with grown-up thoughts as I looked
   At the tattered shoes and gown,
"If you do not know what trouble is
   "No little one knows in town."

Then I thought again, beyond the clothes,
   But I did not answer her,
(For she was fast asleep just then)
   "Trouble is sin, my dear."

Then I thank thee, Heavenly Father,
   My little one's heart is free
From knowledge of that which curses man,
   And keeps them away from Thee.

MY SPELLING BOOK.

I have the queerest spelling book
  That ever you did see;
It wouldn't do for every one,
  But answers well for me.

Mine's not like other spelling books,
  Though it is bound in cloth;
It's not a dictionary,
  But still it does for both.

Its leaves are pink, and when I wish
  They open wide for me;
When moistened by my lips
  They yield correct orthography

When I get mixed on e's and i's
  And would put s for c,
I only need to call on it,
It spells the words for me.

And so it is with c and k
  And l and ll;
The combinations I don't know
  My little book can tell.

And k for c and a for o
  And w and u,
No matter what the trouble is,
  It straightens them out true.

My speller is a roly-poly
  Book of pink and white;

Its covers are of rich, rich brown,
  Its top as black as night.

And strange to say my little book
  Can think as well as walk.
I only have to treat it right
  To hear it laugh and talk.

Oh, how I miss my little book
  When I sit up to write,
What with vowels and diphthongs
  I am distracted quite.

I could not more distressful feel
  Nor tangled up could be,
Than when I'm from my spelling book,
  Or she's away from me.

MARGUERITE SNOW.

I will tell you a story of long ago,
Of my sweetheart, little Marguerite Snow.
We played on the sands by the wide, wide sea,
And I loved her and she loved me,
And we were as happy as we could be.

My Marguerite's eyes were very bright,
And her cheeks were always pink and white;
Her breath was like a baby's sweet,
And I thought she had the prettiest feet,
And our happiness was quite complete,

Her hair was black as a charcoal pit,
And she used to let me fondle it.
Her lips were pink and her teeth were pearls,
And they looked like buds beneath her curls;
And she was the fairest of all the girls.

Her dainty chin was my delight,
And her hands (as soft as baby's, quite)
Were the first to soothe my aches and pains
And to wash away my crimson stains,
And wipe from my eyes the tear-drop rains.

And so we played by the ocean wave,
I thought her fair and she thought me brave;
And we never dreamed that anything
Could cloud our love like a day in spring,
Or set our affections wandering.

But that was oh, so long ago,
We played in the sands in the summer glow;

I will tell you a story of long ago,
Of my sweetheart, little Marguerite Snow.

A boat was tied by the sea that day.
And in it I drifted far away
From her side forever and ever to stay.

An ocean of years is rolling now
Between me and my Marguerite Snow,
But its easy to cross with memory,
For I loved her and she loved me,
In those old days by the blue, blue sea.

THE EVERGREEN SHORE.

Oh, come, my daughter, come with me, to the coasts of evergreen;
Where the broad Pacific laves the shore, and the tall white ships are seen.
Where snow-capped mountains pierce the skies by the side of crystal lakes,
And the wind among the balsam boughs celestial music makes.
Where the gold and silver mountains ring with the miner's pick and spade,
And the water fowl skims on the lake and the deer leaps in the glade.

Oh, come where Puget Sound winds in among a thousand isles,
Where cots and villages nestling stand, and bounteous nature smiles.
Where the tall fir trees make green the tide as it ebbs among the hills,
And mountain lakes pour out their floods in a hundred tumbling rills.
Where cities fair with their hum and stir beside their busy bays,
Send out their ships with steam and sail in many ocean ways.

Oh, come to the fields of Washington, where grows the golden wheat,
And where in the iron mountain's breast the coal rests 'neath our feet;
And the sawmills hum and the canners come with their treasures of the deep.

And the soft winds in the evergreens sing, lulling us to sleep.

Oh, come where the sun bathes in the west when the daylight hours grow late;
Where the lion of the sea basks warm by the side of the Golden Gate.
And the gray gulls scream in mad delight as the ocean ships go out,
At their table spread with lavish hand on the evening waves about.

Oh, come where the salmon leaps with glee in the glorious summer sun,
And flashes his silver armor bright in the vigor of his fun.
Where the halibut in the peaceful calm of his ocean pasture deep,
Jerks taught the line of the fisherman with the vim of his mighty leap.

Oh, come where the palm trees fringe the shores of the mighty Golden State,
And the grapes and oranges hang rich and the hungry pickers wait,
Or where the walrus churns the sea and blows his trumpet loud,
While the bright-eyed, furry-coated seal the Alaska islands crowd.
Or Mt. St. Elias' towering peak is mirrored in the sea
Where the mighty whale makes the ocean boil like a monster pot of tea.
Where the icebergs float on the Arctic stream, like crystal mountains bright,
Or mighty ghosts with silent tread glide by in the misty night.

Come where the stream of Oregon from the mighty
    mountains flows,
Among the fields and happy homes where the prune
    and apple grows,
And where the grain and grass grow high by the side
    of the winding stream,
And in their plenteous comfort there the sheep and
    cattle dream.
Or where the mighty Columbia pours out its mountain
    flood,
To buffet back with sweeping hands the foaming
    ocean rude.

Oh, come with me to the gladsome isle where the
    royal city stands,
Or where the Frazer river flows down over its golden
    sands,
Where the Union Jack floats over fields as rich as
    Eden was;
And offers, free from disease and woe, an enchanted
    home to us.

Oh, come, come, come, my daughter, dear, to the
    coasts of evergreen,
Where Nature fair the whole year through in a ver-
    dant robe is seen;
And the soft Chinook with gentle touch comes out of
    the warm southwest
And draws for all a rich supply from Nature's boun-
    teous breast.

Oh, come, then, come, and make our home where a
    soft and gentle clime
Makes the blood glide smoothly through ones veins
    and the pulses beat in time;

Where everything makes glad the heart and rests the
    weary eye,
And we can live in joy and peace while the happy days
    go by.

THE HOMESICK PROSPECTOR.

Oh, lady of the Golden State,
    With kindness smiling in your face;
    With eye of blue and form of grace,
Can I forget though frowning fate
    Has lead me far, oh, far away?

Can I forget the cooling cup
    You gave me on that weary day,
    I plodded lone along the way?
My lips were longing for the sup,
    A little deed not soon forgot.

The way has long and weary been,
    I sought thy bars Mokelumne,
    Or washed the sands of Tuelumne,
I've many lonely moments seen,
    Far from thy shores of evergreen.

The world is all a snowdrift here;
    From Tia Juana, San Joaquin,
    Or Mono I shall never wean,
Tulare, Tule all, all are dear,
    In this snow bound New England home.

Why did the old man ever roam
    (Oh, fair Kaweah and Tahoe)
    From evergreen to endless snow,
Thus backward from his sunset home,
    To pine unceasingly for thee?

Life will a salty pillar be,
    Chehalem, Klamath, Coquille,

Labish, Umpqua and Owyhee
And Walla Walla, Nestache,
  For the old man so far away.

Sylvan Shannitch and Wapato,
  Chehalis and fair Pen d'Oreille,
  That I from thee so far should stray,
Where thunders roll and cyclones blow;
  The old man will be back again.

Multnomah, Samish, Yakima,
  Doswallips, tumbling Quillaute,
  None shall my love for thee dispute.
Whatcom, Chelan and Willapa,
  Thy placid bosoms I would float.

Nicola, Tumtum, Chilukweyuk,
  Stikine and Illecillewaet,
  Skeena, Sumas and Lillooet,
Once more I'd bend my winding track
  To thee for yellow hidden dust.

Even Alaska's far Yukon,
  Winding Kowak or cold Naatak,
  Or blue and sleeping Nushagak,
Were fairer than the frozen sun
  Which shivers o'er this world of snow.

The old homestead is not the same,
  About it nothing quite so dear
  As the warm hearts who brought me here;
Nothing familiar but the name,
  With fifty years on me and it.

Love cannot drive the gloom away,
  I long to hear the breaker's roar

Upon the ever vernal shore;
The afternoon of life I'd stay
    Where gently blows the soft Chinook.

I long thy mountains near to be,
    Where wind their deep and dreamy shades,
    Sierra Nevadas and Cascades,
Shining in glittering sheen for me,
    A wall 'gainst predatory frosts.

I'm coming, coasts of evergreen,
    Prepare my cabin by the bay,
    Where leaps the salmon in his play;
Nieces and nephews cannot wean;
    By thee the old man's dust shall lie.

Oh, the roses of Tacoma.

*THE ROSES OF TACOMA.

Oh, the roses of Tacoma, how they glorify the hills;
How their fragrant breath ascending the very ether fills;
How the Junetime speaks in accents pink and white and blush and cream,
While the air is fraught with incense like a sweet Elysian dream.

Oh, the roses of Tacoma, how they grace the sombre walls;
How they cling about the porches where the wooing hammock calls;
How the petals falling, falling with the glowing tints of dawn,
And in waxen colors spattered paint the pallette of the lawn.

Oh, the roses of Tacoma, how their damask blushes woo,
While the lazy laden zephyrs mid their bowers are creeping through,
Stealing here and there while wandering an attar-scented kiss,
Which whispers where the zephyrs go of ecstasy of bliss.

Oh, the roses of Tacoma, moist with dew at early morn,

---

*What is said of the roses of Tacoma may as truthfully be said of the roses of Victoria, Seattle, or any other Pacific Coast city. The Evergreen Shore is a land of roses from June to January.

Culled by dainty waxen fingers some soft corsage to
    adorn;
There conspiring with the glowing of fair cheeks to
    overthrow
Slaves, who, with their senses raptured, to the meshes
    willing go.

Oh, the roses of Tacoma, sweet physicians they have
    come
To the bedside of the weary, in the wards, from friends
    and home;
Loaning to wan cheeks their blushes, bringing sun-
    light to the eye,
And in accents soft, refreshing, bid disease and death
    to fly.

Oh, the roses of Tacoma, in their arbors of delight,
How they paint the day with blushes and perfume the
    sleeping night,
Till the world a bed of roses with its witching odors
    seems,
And their blushes and their fragrance fill the sleep and
    waking dreams.

UPS AND DOWNS.

Life is a teeter, up and down we go;
However skyward we ascend we must come down, we
 know;
And so it is, with ups and downs we with our neighbors share;
First lightly floating up with joy, then burdened down
 with care.

When he is up then we are down and vice versa he;
Continually in upper air no one can hope to be.
Our neighbor sinking brings us up, he rising brings
 us down,
While we can never rise again until we strike the
 ground.

And so, while we are mixing up the sadness with the
 joy
We should not let our sinking hopes our happiness
 destroy,
But gather in our settling feet the strength we have to
 spare;
Then when we strike the ground a push will lift us in
 the air.

HOW THE GRANDMAS GOT IN.

It was late one day when the grandmas tried
At heaven's gate to get inside;
They hadn't the least idea that they
Would be asked outside of Paradise to stay,
But Peter was gone to bathe his wings
In the sea of glass, and other things,
And had left an angel, maybe John,
Or Lot, or Isaac, or some other one,
To tend the gate while he was away,
And Ruth, with the baby angels at play,
Was so busy of course she couldn't know
What was going on at the gates below.

Well, strange to tell, and sad, though true,
The angel wouldn't let the grandmas through,
And told them that they must stay outside
(Though some of them sat right down and cried)
Until he found if the things were true
He had heard of them from one or two.
He said there were some in heaven that day
Who had almost been obliged to stay
Outside the pearly gates, because
Of something they had done that was
Just brought about by these grandmas.

The cases the angels had in mind
Where something like these, when he went to find
The ones who had almost been too bad
To get inside, and it made him sad.
There was angel Tom, who grandmama
Had hid in her room away from ma,
Who was after him with a slipper shoe,

For telling a story that wasn't true;
Then there was pretty angel Nell,
Who was naughty and wouldn't take her pill,
And grandma, meaning well enough,
Said "grandma's pet shan't take the stuff."

Besides there were many other things
Which had come to heaven on angels' wings,
Of how the grandmamas had spoiled
And "cruel" papas and mammas foiled,
Until some of the children had almost gone
To the bad for wicked things they'd done,
When a little correcting would have kept
From sins for which their parents wept.

Well, while the grandmas sat and cried,
A little kind angel peeped down and spied
The white heads, bent in trembling grief,
With no one to come to their relief,
And when he saw their cheeks were wet,
His own grandma he couldn't forget,
And quietly he slipped away,
To Ruth and the little ones at play.

Sweet Ruth listened with surprise,
When she saw the tear drops in his eyes.
Then quickly to the portals went,
And over the jasper capstones bent,
And looking to the ground below,
Saw the heads bowed down as white as snow.
Her voice was very soft and sad,
As she whispered, "oh, too bad, too bad!
"They never could have known 'twas wrong,
"They were so old and loved so strong."

Then the children angels each begin:
"They're grandmamas! do let them in!"
And Ruth, with warm and throbbing heart,
Slipped the bars and bolts of the gate apart,
While the little ones gathered round in glee,
With joy their kindly smiles to see,
And thus they lead the grandmas through
Into Paradise, where the skies are blue,
And John and Isaac they never knew.

And when Peter found what Ruth had done,
He said he wouldn't have kept out one;
And again, when he laid the key on the shelf:
"I had a dear grandma myself."
While every one sang, it was plain to see
That they were happy as they could be
To welcome the grandmamas inside,
And not one tried his delight to hide.
And that was the way, though it was quite late,
That the grandmas got through the pearly gate.

ROSES IN THE PATH.

The maiden fair with the golden hair,
   When she threw her roses away,
With her princess air and her raiment rare,
   Had never a thought to-day
(As the buds and blossoms, drooping low,
   By the dusty pathway fell)
That they, with their blushes from above,
   Sweet joy to a heart would tell.

But so it was, and my little room,
   With their royal glow grew bright,
While they, thirsty, supped from my drinking cup,
   And bloomed for my delight.
For a happy week I tended them,
   And dreamed, while I gazed with joy,
That my little room in the noisy flat
   Was some palace far away.

And the maiden fair with the golden hair
   Passed on and never dreamed
That for her rejected flowers to-day
   A life far brighter seemed.
But I thought when I gathered them from the dust,
   There are joys in every day,
And happy are we if we find delight
   In what others throw away.

*CAPILANO.

Oh Capilano, how I sigh
  For thee, my mountain stream,
While on these burning sands I lie,
  And of thy fountains dream.

Lost in the desert wandering,
  No sheltering shadow nigh,
With parched lips and fevered brain,
  I feel that I must die.

So as the bloody sunlight glares
  Across the desert waste,
And drifts below the glittering sands,
  I long of thee to taste.

And as I lie my body down,
  To toss in troubled sleep,
I dream of gray and moss grown rocks,
  Down which thy waters leap.

I dream of shadows dense and deep
  Beneath the evergreens,
Where, gazing in thy looking glass,
  The partridge dips and preenes,
While waiting for her mate who drums
  Upon the mossy trunk
A challenge to his feathery foe,
  While he with love is drunk.

---

*The stream from which the city of Vancouver, B. C., takes its water.

I dream of gray and moss-grown rocks down which thy waters leap.

I dream, while stretched upon the sands
    And seeking fevered rest,
Of where thy bubbling springs burst from
    The mountain's icy breast,
Of where the sunbeams chase the snows
    From off the rugged peaks,
Down where thy brawling tumbling stream
    The deepest shadow seeks.

I wake, the sun creeps threatening up
    From out its sandy bed,
And with the night, I find my dreams
    Of Capilano fled.
But still I waking dream of thee,
    While through the sands I wade,
And seek, with burning, quivering eyes
    The green oasis shade.

And even though I sit beneath
    The palm trees' sheltering boughs,
My thought leaps up, and o'er the sea
    To Capilano goes.
And there would I with ecstasy
    Fly with my wooing dream,
To where the gushing fountain plays
    From Capilano's stream.

THE NEW HOUSE.

I hate you and all your polished walls
And massive doors of precious woods.
There is only one redeeming feature in you,
With all your glittering, glaring elegance,
And that a whispering, longing thought of her
For whom I dreamed to raise your massive domes.
The funeral silence of your mossy carpets
Makes my heart as chill as your cold stones;
As sad I wander up and down your halls alone;
For she is gone and earth and you and I are empty.

I brought her yonder where the elm tree droops,
She planted with her own dear hands
So long ago; and roses bloomed on face and field;
And sushine shone in heaven and eye,
And brightened everthing with hope and joy.

The mossy cabin she delighted in,
The forest shades of green and gray beyond,
Even the toil of clearing off the massive trees
Was entertaining, and to her had its delight.
Her dimpled hands and face were often painted
With the char of sticks she piled upon
The glowing fires, which ate the shade away
And let the hoe and sunlight to the willing soil.

The busy years flew by, the "old house" stood
Where once the cabin's mossy logs were piled.
Her elm tree shaded round the porch,
And children played and sang about the place,
Still, she was e'er the faithful guardian,
And when the calls of business took me far away.

She bore the burdens of the home alone,
And life more full of toil and cares
Than what the world calls pleasures,
She lived through all the years with few complaints.

Her girlhood feet had pressed the velvet,
And frescoed walls had looked upon her then,
But now the garden soil clung to her dainty shoes.
Her little hands were not as soft as when
They handled only cunning needle work or lace.
Necessity, that thorough but mysterious teacher,
Drew his impassable lines about her home,
And made a world of it, at least for her.

The moments passed, and while I dreamed.
The hand of Time sprinkled the frosts of years
Upon my head, and to my joints poured in
The curdled oil of age with stealthy hand.
Deceiving me, he kept her just as fair,
Nor meddled with her velvet face or hair.
The only sign she gave that time or toil or care
Had touched her, was now and then a sigh.

Frowning adversity had meek submission taught;
And then upon us smiled one day prosperity.
The old house 'neath the elm tree's spreading shade
(When I upon our new good fortune thought)
Seemed mean and poor and cramped.
And then I thought to rear a home for her
More like the one she left to come to me.
She said, when I the subject broached to her:
"We have been happy here, the place is dear,
"And here the children have around us grown
"To men and women, and gone out
"The world to see, and this to them is home."
But still, I thought I did it all for her,
And so your towers and pillars grew.

And you, new house, were thus completed.
The upholsterer and the cabinet maker came,
And artists hung your frescoed walls
With bits of silent nature face and form.
We walked about your halls and stairways
Like children lost in some strange wilderness,
Until one day she tired grew and pale
And lay her down to rest, but not in thee, new house,
For with a weary smile she asked me
To carry her to her own little room,
Where in the elm tree she could hear the robin sing.

We bore her gently home across the field
And left you here, a monument to pride.
"Oh, I am tired, and just want to rest,"
She said, when we, with sadly bending heads
Inquired what we could do for her.
And so she went to sleep in her own little room,
To never more behold the marble halls
I built for her when she had worn her life away.
And when I knew that we could never wake her
It came to me how void of recreations
And how circumscribed her life had been.
And then a thought of bitterness came in;
That she had never been rewarded for her cares,
And had been snatched away from tardy joys,
Which came too late to cheer the life
Which she had spent for others' comforts.

Defrauded, all her life of cheering recreations,
And filled her world with sacrifice and self-denials.
I take no joy in you, new house;
You make my days more lonely and bring up
The thought of how she closed her weary life,
Not with delights and comforts here,
But with the silence of mysterious death.

Lady of the Golden State.

There are more pleasant places, and to others
I will leave the task of waking up your corridors
While I repine beneath our spreading elm
(By which her youthful days were bright)
And meditate upon the promised glorious home,
Built by more generous hands than you,
And where she waits for me among the scenes
Where mysteries are all revealed, and sacrifice
Not unevenly distributed on gentle shoulders.
Farewell, new house, I can't forsake old friends
For you, and will not hate you when
Your walls are hidden from my sight;
So, as I go where she fell asleep, new house, good
    night.

LADY OR GENTLEMAN.

The lady is the one who has no envy or false pride;
Who always wears a kindly face whatever may betide.
The lady's one who needs not death her sympathies to stir
"To do to others as she would that they should do to "her."

The gentleman's the man who cares for what he says or does
To other people's feelings, as through the world he goes.
The gentleman's the man who can the Lord's commandments keep,
"Rejoice with those who do rejoice and weep with "those who weep."

A lady or a gentleman is one whose heart can move
In sympathy for those around, with God's unselfish love.
No matter how a man may look or what a woman wear,
Their life is hollow as a drum unless God's love is there.

MY OLD VIOLIN.

(A Song.)

Dedicated to my Friend R. S. Yeomans.

Oh, my old violin, my old violin,
To love thee, old friend, is surely no sin;
For we've grown old together mid struggle and strife,
And together we've met all the changes of life.
        Oh, my old violin, my old violin,
        Why shouldn't I love my old violin?

Can I ever forget how you served in the past,
While memory lives and my old life shall last?
How you frightened the ravenous wolf from the door,
And saved my dear wife and our sweet children four?
        Oh, my old violin, my old violin,
        Why shouldn't I love my old violin?

They are gone where the viols of heaven resound,
But the sound of your voice makes my old pulses bound.
While these trembling lips can so hardly repeat
The story, your voice grows forever more sweet.
        Oh, my old violin, my old violin,
        Why shouldn't I love my old violin?

The days of my youth are all vanished and gone
If it were not for you I should be all alone
Then I'll love thee, my friend, whatever they say,
So long as we're kept from our dear ones away.
        Oh, my old violin, my old violin,
        Why shouldn't I love my old violin?

Oh, my old violin, my old violin,
How oft' through the gloom their loved forms I've
    seen,
When you poured out your soul, a balm to my heart;
Oh, my old violin, we never shall part.
        Oh, my old violin, my old violin,
        Why shouldn't I love my old violin?

On Santa Catalina Island.

MISS WISDOM.

Miss Wisdom is a merry lass;
When she peeps in her looking glass
She sees a face, which, though not fair
Of wholesomeness has quite its share.
She's neither handsome, neither plain,
But of her looks cannot complain.
Her eyes are bright, complexion good,
And though she rather smaller would
Prefer her nose, the smile beneath
Shows glistening rows of pearly teeth.
She'll in her charms of form and face
Among her sisters hold her place.

But 'tis not in mere charms of face
That I would sing Miss Wisdom's praise,
But of the things that she can do
That I would stop and write to you:
It will not cause you much surprise
That she when scrubbing never cries,
Does not object to dishes wash,
Or making bread, or serving hash,
But when I try to tell you how
She'll mend a harness, fix a plow,
Or ride a colt or milk a cow,
Has shod a horse herself alone,
Can hitch and drive a team to town,
You'll own that she's resourceful quite,
And able her own way to fight.

Miss Wisdom is a woman, though,
With all her conquests masculine,
And she can handle grill and dough

And ply the needle deft and fine.
The things that she can make and cut
A catalogue I'd give you, but
If I should tell you all she knows
Of cunning things a woman does,
With half an eye you'd surely see
That she was just the girl for me,
And think that she my heart had caught,
With all the winning arts she wrought,
And made of me a lover true,
By subtle passion forced to woo;
But no, Miss Wisdom only crossed
My path, and then in past was lost,
But in my memory linger now
The things of which I write to you.
I speak of gifts which I admire,
And not of passion's thralling fire;
And memories of those remain,
Though her I never see again.
I leave Miss Wisdom, now, with you,
For I have told her story through.
If I again should speak of this
Remind me gently to desist.

THE WIRE'S WAIL.

Wand'ring
  All 'lone;
  Stars shone.
No sound
Around
  Save sighing wind.

But hark!
  Breaks in
  A din.
Humans?
Demons?
  Unearthly revelry.

That strain,
  How drear;
  Not near.
It moans
Across the plain.

Some one
  Talks low
  They go
Close by;
Oh fly!
  This vigil done!

A voice!
  'Tis not!
  Then what?
The wind;
It's trend
  Thankful 'tis so.

That yell
  That moan—
  That groan;
Such cries—
Such sighs:
  They come from hell.

On, on!
  More low
  They flow,
The strain
Will wane
  Hush! they are gone.

Soft strains
  'Ol'yan
  They fan,
Which trill
And thrill
  The soul with awe.

Again
  They roll;
  A pole
To sky
Points high;
  It trembling stands.

'Tis plain;
  Me sees
  The breeze
Grows higher
The wire
  Sings symphonies.

BED TIME.

Sister says its 'leepy time,
Mamma says its bed time,
Papa says it's whiney time,
But I can't see why;
I don't want to go to bed;
I had rather 'tay up late;
I don't like to sit up 'traight,
'Cause it makes me cry.

I ain't 'leepy, not a bit.
I had rather 'tay up yet,
Jus' like big folks, every night—
Talk and read the papers, too;
Then, may be, before I go
Hunt up sumpin' good to eat,
Or some one would bring me sweets,
Just the same as sister Sue.

Curl up here upon the lounge,
Just to hear what people say.
No, no, I don't want to play;
I have been at play all day,
Why I'm keeqin' quite so 'till?
'Cause I'm thinkin' awful hard;
So please wont you go away?

No, I wasn't sound a'leep;
Had my eyes a little s'ut.
Guess you'd s'ut your eyes up tight,
'F you'd kept lookin' at the light.
Never saw the sand man come;
Only got 'ticks in my eyes.

Got to go along to bed?
Mamma, Papa, all, good night.

Now I lay me down to 'leep,
I pray Thee, Lord,
My soul to keep;
If I should die before I wake,
I pray Thee, Lord,
My soul to take.

THE TYPEWRITER GIRL.

(A Song.)

Sung the past of bonnie milkmaid,
   And of maiden raking hay,
With their saucy ringlets flying,
   While on cheeks the dimples play,
But the present has a darling
   As bewitching, every whit,
And before the swift typewriter
   She, the reigning queen, must sit.
     Oh, the pretty, sweet typewriter,
       With her quiet business ways,
     How she stirs the world around her
       In these rushing latter days.

Do but see her, as she swiftly
   Glides along the busy street,
In her mind mother and sister,
   Naught but business in her feet.
Like a gleam of springtime sunshine
   Flits she through the office door,
Softening all the grim surroundings
   As they never were before.

See her waxen fingers patter
   O'er the keys like darting birds,
While the flashing types are spelling
   Out the swiftly flying words.
And the brown eyes keenly peering,
   Neath the thatch of sable curls,
Picture of industry witching,
   Oh, those sweet typewriter girls. .

Willingly she takes the burden,
  Bravely meets the frowning care,
To provide for widowed mother,
  With a courage rich and rare.
Proud to labor for the loved ones,
  Who a father's care have lost.
Yes, we'll sing of our typewriter,
  She's the fairest and the best.

THE FLOWER BUBS.

The hammock swung in the evening breeze,
  While the summer sky hung low,
And the wind harp played in the evergreens
  In drousy cadence slow.
Reclining listless, Rachel slept.
  Till the night awoke the stars,
And the dews crept out on nature's cheeks,
  While his song the cricket jars.

The maiden slept, and her drooping lids
  Robed soft her azure eyes,
And her flowing wealth of brown, brown hair
  O'er the hammock pillow lies.
Her arm of ivory underneath
  Her cheek of peachy down,
While across her wine-red trembling lip
  Her gentle breath is blown.

While Rachel sleeps the flower bubs come,
  And gather round her there,
To choose the colors they will paint
  On fruit and flowers so fair;
A work so deft and delicate
  They find they can't decide,
Until in the hammock slumbering
  Our Rachel they have spied.

Then whispering they gather round
  By Rachel's resting place,
And gaze with rapturous delight
  On the colors of her face.

When they have gazed, and gazed their fill,
  At cheek and brow and lip,
And e'en beneath the eyelids soft,
  They down from the hammock slip.

"We've found the color for the rose,
  "The peach and the apple flower,"
  (They shout, as they gather down below)
  "And need to seek no more.
"The lily we'll paint like Rachel's brow,
  "The violet (like her eye
"And the soft, kind-eyed forget-me-not)
  "As blue as the summer sky.
"The rose of June and the apple ripe,
  "And autumn's luscious peach,
"The blush of the slumbering maiden's cheek
  "Suggests a tint for each.
"The plum, and the berries hid away,
  "Which peep from their summer bed,
"We'll paint like Rachel's trembling lips,
  "With brushes pink and red."

Then the maiden stirred, and the hammock swayed,
  And the flower bubs slipped away
To their studios and pots of paint,
  To mix their colors gay;
And while they toiled among the flowers,
  And berries and apple trees,
Our Rachel never knew that she
  Suggested the tints for these.

WHERE THE MONEY GOES.

The finance question, certainly's a most engrossing one,
For surely without finances there nothing could be done.
Without the necessary funds how can things move along?
That people haven't got enough is surely very wrong.

They say there isn't money now to do the business on,
And I am sure, without a doubt, that that is true for one,
For now a month or more have I been longing for some cash
To buy a sparkling diamond pin to fasten up my sash.

And I have learned, to-day, for sure where all the money goes,
But why it never comes again is something no one knows.
Of course I cannot bring it back, I only know at most
The money that we need, and cannot have, is lost.

I never knew before to-day, when out for knowledge bent,
And following a simple clew, where all the money went;
But now it is the plainest thing, and troubles me no more;
I only wonder when I think I never knew before.

I met the landlord of the inn who keeps the butcher
   shop
And entertains at his hotel so many guests who stop.
At my salute of "How de do? How's everything to-
   "day?"
"I'm losing money right along," he answered mourn-
   fully.

I saw the shoemaker, he said, "I'm losing money
   "fast,"
As from a shoe with vicious jerk he pulled a fractious
   last.
The baker man I found as well was losing money,
   too,
In spite of all the plans he made and all that he could
   do.

The drayman and the farmer and the carpenter as
   well—
The blacksmith and the merchant, all the same sad
   story tell—
How they're losing money every day, in spite of
   everything,
In the summer and the autumn and the winter and
   the spring.

And so you see, it's plain to me where all the money
   goes;
It's lost, is why that it's so scarce, now everybody
   knows.
The only wonder in it all, no money's ever found,
While so many men and women are losing all
   around,
And finding the lost money it is time we had begun,
Then there would be a plenty to do the business on.

MY PATRONS.

My patrons were not kings and queens;
I was unheeded by the rich,
They stopped not for my humble plea;
And if I found a place at all,
It was in warm and lowly hearts.
A foundling at the door of hearts,
The humble kindly took me in;
The proud rejected and despised;
They sought a child of nobler birth,
On whom their favors to bestow.
The poor, their humble hearths and hearts
Divided with the stranger child,
And trusted that the source from which
They drew upon for their supply,
Would not grow less than their demands;
And but for their responsive hearts
I should in solitude have died,
While humbly crying at their doors.
May Heaven bless the hearts that beat
In sympathy not fixed by pelf.

www.ingramcontent.com/pod-product-compliance
Lightning Source LLC
Chambersburg PA
CBHW031955230426

43672CB00010B/2161